MARXISM AND THE EXISTENTIALISTS

RAYMOND ARON

A Clarion Book

PUBLISHED BY SIMON AND SCHUSTER

The First Dialogue, Second Dialogue, and Introduction were translated by
Helen Weaver. In the Third Dialogue, "The Impact of Marxism in the
Twentieth Century" was translated by Robert Addis, and "Sartre's Marxism"
was translated by John Weightman.

"Sartre's Marxism" originally appeared in *Encounter*, June, 1965. Copyright ©
1965 by Encounter Ltd. Reprinted with permission.

"The Impact of Marxism in the Twentieth Century" is reprinted from MARXISM
IN THE MODERN WORLD (Hoover Institution Publications), edited by Milorad
M. Drachkovitch, with the permission of the publishers, Stanford University
Press. Copyright © 1965 by the Board of Trustees of the Leland Stanford Junior
University.

Contents

Introduction

The five essays included in this book were written at three different times: the first in 1946, immediately after the liberation, the next two in 1955, after the death of Stalin and before Khrushchev's denunciation of the cult of personality, and the last two in 1964, when the cold war as well as the controversy among French intellectuals was beginning to abate. The first essay was written prior to the breaking off of youthful friendships; it more or less coincides with the end of certain alliances formed during the war and the resistance. The last four mark the decline of passions and polemics.

Nevertheless it seems to me that despite differences of tone, these studies have a common purpose: a dialogue between the existentialists and the Marxists as interpreted by a third speaker, namely, the author of the book, not forgetting that the existentialists are sometimes divided into two schools, that of Jean-Paul Sartre on the one hand and that of Maurice Merleau-Ponty on the other.

Why have I been so interested in this dialogue? Why have I felt the need to take part in it? Political motives have not been the only ones, and probably they have not even been decisive.

In Germany, after 1930, I began my intellectual career with a reflection on Marxism. An "advanced thinker," like most of the intellectuals who came out of the Jewish bourgeoisie, I wanted to make a philosophical critique of my political convictions, which I felt to be naïve, dictated by the milieu, with no other foundation than spontaneous preferences or antipathies.

This critique consisted, and still consists, of two elements: a comparison of the historical perspectives opened by the Marxism of Marx with the actual development of modern society; and an exploration of the relation between history and the historian, between society and the one who interprets it, between the historicity of collective institutions and that of the individual.

The situation during the thirties differed profoundly from that of the sixties. Thirty years ago the capitalists were not far from believing in the truth of the Marxist prophecies. I have spoken somewhere, in connection with these prophecies, of a *catastrophic optimism*. Non-Marxists did not retain the optimism, the radiant image of the post-capitalist regime or of the planned economy, but inclined toward catastrophism. For my part, I did not rule out catastrophes—on the contrary, the rise of national socialism made it impossible to be unaware of their imminence—but even then it seemed to me impossible to account for the events of the century within the framework of classical Marxism (that Marxism which the Second International, following Engels, had codified and vulgarized).

The arguments that had led me to the conclusion that Marxism was not true (although I wished with all my heart that it was) are, I admit, hopelessly commonplace. Even then I was already determined not to be afraid of facts, even those that are cited by reactionaries. The conformism of the left was just as disagreeable to me as the conformism of the right. Even in those remote days I wondered why planning should automatically be the prerogative of the left and the mechanism of the market that of the right.

The evidence that prevented me, in spite of myself, from becoming a Marxist, nobody today any longer denies. The so-called capitalist regime, that is, the regime defined by private ownership of the instruments of production and the mechanisms of the market, does not bring about the pauperization of the masses, it does not spontaneously create the division of the social body into a minority of exploiters and a mass of the exploited, it does not dig its own grave. When a country with a capitalist regime undergoes a crisis, the uprooted masses—nonproletarian masses and partly even proletarian masses—are just as apt to join a nationalist movement as a movement of internationalist inspiration. In 1914 the German workers had proved to be just as patriotic as the French workers. From 1930 to 1933 in the Weimar Republic nationalism had once again stifled the so-called proletarian or revolutionary conscience.

This evidence suggested a historical vision essentially different from that of classical Marxism. Neither the primacy of one type of cause nor the conception of capitalism as a historic totality was, in my eyes, consistent with reality, as soon as this reality was examined without prejudice. Neither the war of 1914 nor the outbreaks of fascism were the effects or expressions of "capitalism," transfigured, for purposes of demonstration, into a mysterious and omnipresent monster. The division of humanity into sovereign states, into separate and self-conscious nations, had preceded capitalism and would survive it. Furthermore, socialism, to the extent that it meant state ownership and control of the instruments of production, would inevitably reinforce nationalism in the twofold sense of the state's desire for independence or power and of popular involvement in the political community. Thirty years ago I was already inclined to suspect that all socialism was national (although all national socialism need not be National Socialist, if Hitler's regime is taken as a model).

Having renounced, regretfully but once and for all, a "monistic" or all-inclusive view of contemporary evolution, I was resigned to making decisions that were free and attended by risk, not blindly, but without any precise or certain knowledge of the future—that knowledge of the end of history which would give one's commitment the sanction of an ultimate truth. Furthermore, the "pluralistic" nature of the historical reality as well as the plurality of values makes our choices both ambiguous and dramatic. No regime simultaneously accomplishes everything to which we aspire. Beginning with Marxism, I arrived at the tragic existentialism of Max Weber. In the thirties as I witnessed, almost in despair, the decadence of the French nation and the corruption of the democracies, I wondered whether one day it would be necessary to choose between the salvation of my country and the preservation of freedom.

This philosophy, to which, in my *Introduction à la philosophie de l'histoire*, I gave an exaggeratedly pathetic expression (the less one has known of suffering, the more one is sometimes given to the tragic style), was in no way *irrationalist*. On the contrary, it was, and still is, as I interpret it, essentially rationalist, but, to use Sartre's terminology, its rationality is *analytic* or *scientific*. It has nothing to do with historical Reason, if the latter is conceived as a reconciliation between subject and object, between men and their works, as the assurance that global history ultimately obeys a rationality of which individual actors are the unconscious agents.

This conception was the culmination of what I referred to above as the second object of my reflection on Marxism: the relation of historical man to history, which is both internal and external to him—internal because the objective mind is present in him, external because he feels miserable and helpless in the face of the forces that are unleashed during periods of upheaval. This way of thinking might have been called dialectical if this term, in the current usage of the Marxists, had not implied both *totality* (or totalization) and knowledge of the *end* (the end of prehistory, if not of history itself).

Before the war of 1939, or rather before 1917, this discussion was essentially German. Of all Marxist schools before 1914, the German school was the most prestigious. The Russian school did not deny its debt to its Germanic masters. Even in 1903, when he wrote *What Is to Be Done?*, Lenin invoked Karl Kautsky to justify the role of the intellectuals, who were alone capable of saving the workers from the temptation and facility of trade unionism, from syndical vindication *hic et nunc*, without awareness of or desire for a historic mission. The philosophy of Marx, precisely because of its intrinsic ambiguity—is the movement of history governed by laws comparable to the laws of nature, or is it the result of a free, and hence to a certain extent unpredictable, response of men to a situation?—has always lent itself to many interpretations, some of which are more convincing than others if you follow the rules of historical criticism, but all of which, strictly speaking, are tolerable: a *Kantian Marxism,* if you assume socialism to be a moral objective determined by the conscience in the face of the capitalist reality; a *Hegelian Marxism,* whose origins are in the *Phenomenology of Mind* more than they are in the *Philosophy of Right;* and a positivist or *scientific Marxism,* which is more or less Hegelianized by the inclusion of a dialectic of nature. All these versions of Marxism have in common the fact that they are *humanistic,* provided we understand this vague term to imply an affirmation that "man is for man the supreme being" and that the motive and ambition of socialism is the fulfillment of man, however indefinite may be the nature or essence of man.

The revolution of 1917 created an additional uncertainty. It is possible to interpret Marxism-Leninism in voluntarist terms; in fact, this is even the most normal interpretation of the Bolshevik enterprise which, in contempt of the orthodox doctrine, seized power in a country where the working class was a minority and where capitalism had not yet reached maturity. But, for politically understandable motives, the Bolsheviks maintained both an *objectivist theory* of the evolution of history and a *practice* which was alien to this theory and, so to speak, *systematically opportunistic.*

Now, the philosophers, historians, or sociologists who supported the Soviet cause or sympathized with it wavered, according to circumstances and their temperaments, between two attitudes. Either they faithfully repeated the platitudes constantly being imposed by the orthodoxy of the state, no matter how false or even absurd this orthodoxy was, or they looked to the Marxism of Marx, and especially of the young Marx, for a subtler version of their faith. Georg Lukács' book *History and Class Consciousness* is responsible for this return to sources. It contains most of the themes of the ideological or sociological disputes which stirred socialist circles in Weimar Germany. Repudiated by the author himself a few years later, its Marx-

ism is both Hegelian and existential: Hegelian because it tries
to grasp the dialectical unity of subject and object, of history
as a whole and the class which becomes conscious of this history
before surpassing it; existential because the condition imposed
on man by the capitalist regime, the depersonalization of social
relations, the alienation of man in things, characterizes reality
and at the same time inherently contains a criticism of this
reality.

This kind of Marxism has never been accepted by the Bolsheviks, and it is still not accepted today, although in eastern
Europe there is some evidence of a greater tolerance toward
and an increased interest in the young Marx and in Hegelian-
existential Marxism.

This subtle Marxism (let us so designate the Marxism which
rejects the objectivistic and naturalistic philosophy of Engels
and the simplifications of diamat, and puts the emphasis on the
dialectic between the subjective and the objective, between the
situation and the men, and which denounces capitalism because of the condition which it imposes on men) does not
logically imply any political stance. It may justify the adoption
of Marxism-Leninism, in which case it constitutes a personal,
semiclandestine interpretation of the officially accepted dogma.
It may also be combined with a sympathy for the Soviet cause
without membership in the Communist party; it may also lead
to hostility toward Marxism-Leninism without rejection of the
Marxist inspiration. After 1945 the French existentialists Jean-
Paul Sartre and Maurice Merleau-Ponty took up the search for
a subtle Marxism which the Third Reich had interrupted in
Germany. For my own part, I was plagued by two questions,
one political, the other moral. Once the historical vision of
Marxism has been refuted by history itself, what place is the
individual to assume in the evolution of modern society? What
is the approach which leads to a commitment that is not true,
but reasonable?

I am afraid the reader will occasionally become irritated by
the contrast between the subtlety of the controversies and the

relative simplicity of the questions, by the translation of political positions into a somewhat abstruse philosophical language. At times I myself question the significance of these disputes. However, the French existentialists have occupied too important a place in the literary life of France over the past twenty years to give us the right to dismiss even the most vulnerable part of their work. Besides, and most importantly, their way of thinking is not an expression of French provincialism. Other writers or thinkers throughout the world have been seduced by the same arguments, have fallen victim to the same sophisms.

What was the issue, between 1945 and 1956 (the date of Khrushchev's speech to the Twentieth Congress of the Russian Communist party), that divided French intellectuals—Communists, more or less sympathetic non-Communists, and anti-Communists? The Communists blindly followed the party line, which in turn conformed to instructions from Moscow. According to the occasion, advanced socialists or "fellow travelers"—for example, Sartre and his friends—were denounced to the indignant masses as "objective" allies of capitalism and imperialism or, on the contrary, welcomed, not without reservations, as fighters for peace and democracy.

Sartre and Merleau-Ponty, without ever deviating from their anti-anti-Communism, and without ever joining the Communist party, hesitated between several attitudes. In 1947 Sartre tried to form an organization which would have fallen somewhere between Communism, which was unacceptable to free minds, and a bourgeois type of socialism, which was too prosaic to satisfy a revolutionary desire. The failure of this project brought him closer to the Communist party, with whom he collaborated in affiliated organizations like the peace movement. Merleau-Ponty always remained outside of parties and kept away from all properly political activity, but in *Humanisme et Terreur,* he attributed the Communist enterprise with a historic privilege which he denied it a few years later in *Les Aventures de la dialectique,* after the Korean war and a reappraisal of his own philosophy.

The sociologist will be inclined to give a simple explanation of these hesitations, these half-joinings and half-leavings. Prevented by their ideas and the decline of their country from resigning themselves to a bourgeois democracy, and repelled by the ideological despotism of Communism, these thinkers had no country other than the country of their dream, a Communism which was different from that of the Soviet Union at the time of Stalin or even of Khrushchev. These homeless intellectuals, who belonged to neither of the two camps in the cold war, argued endlessly about the exact nuance that suited their abstention.

Personally, I objected less to the political attitude of either —I sometimes found it unreasonable, but never unworthy (whereas in Sartre's eyes my own attitude was not unreasonable but was unworthy)—than to the philosophical justification of decisions which I considered personal and arbitrary. Merleau-Ponty, at the time he was writing *Humanisme et Terreur*, and Sartre, after 1945, wanted, if not to derive their political commitment from their philosophy, at least to show that this commitment could not be separated from their philosophy. In these studies I try to show that, on the contrary, there is no necessary connection between the two.

What are the essential arguments on which French existentialists tried to base "the historical privilege of the Communist enterprise"? The first, which is found in *Humanisme et Terreur* as well as in the writings of Sartre, refers to the *intention* of the historical movement that calls itself Marxist-Leninist. In spite of everything, this movement is motivated by a plan of total liberation, whereas in a sense the other parties are resigned to injustices of a kind that reforms may improve but not radically transform. This argument contradicts a celebrated thesis of Marx in the Preface to *A Contribution to the Critique of Political Economy*. If we must judge societies according to what they are and not according to what they pretend to be, why should the Communist enterprise be defined by its alleged goal rather than by the regimes to which, temporarily at least, it has given birth?

The second argument, related to the first, is that the failure of the Communist enterprise signifies the failure of historical Reason itself. This argument is also easy to refute. Why, assuming that human history must either end happily or remain a senseless turmoil, should the crucial experience occur in the middle of the twentieth century, in a country in no way marked for this sublime role? The true believer, won over by the idealism of the revolutionary parties, feels robbed of hope on the day when these parties have been defeated by their victory, that is, when they have revealed themselves as similar to those they have replaced.

Beyond these two arguments the paths of Merleau-Ponty and Sartre diverge. The first sought the foundation of his Marxism in an actual experience, that of the proletariat; the second sought it in a decision, that of the party which transforms the class which, as such, is a "passive seriality," into a group, that is, into an action. With the perspective of the past ten years, and after reading *La Critique de la raison dialectique,* I would make a somewhat different interpretation of the controversy that went on between the two friends in 1955–56. The difference of opinion was philosophically more profound than I suggested, and Merleau-Ponty was more right than I believed.

Sartre, in spite of everything, never transcended the Cartesian duality as reinterpreted by Husserl. The Sartrian consciousness is solitary, self-translucid, and alienated in matter, and as a result of uniqueness, each man becomes the enemy of every other. It is only by revolt, in violent action, that men together escape solitude and inhumanity, pending their mutual recognition. The rejection of intermediary situations underlies both the Sartrian dualism and the critique made of it by Merleau-Ponty.

Perhaps the most characteristic trait of the Marxism of the French existentialists (and of Lukács too, for that matter) is their indifference to the economic and perhaps even to the sociological problems of Marxism. It is as if Sartre, as well as Merleau-Ponty, had been less concerned with the content of the socio-economic theories of Marx or the Marxists than with the reconciliation of a philosophy of personal destiny with a philosophy of collective salvation by history.

Merleau-Ponty, who died before he completed his work, seemed to have drifted away from these historico-political controversies and returned to the ultimate questions of philosophy, but he had agreed that the objective examination of opposing regimes preceded commitment and formed a foundation for it. Sartre, on the other hand, remained faithful to himself, and one looks in vain, in *La Critique de la raison dialectique*, for a motive of any kind—economic, social, or political—for preferring a Soviet regime to a regime of the Western type. He announces with a dogmatism that is unconsciously naïve that the analysis in *Das Kapital* is so completely and obviously true that any commentary is useless and could only serve to weaken its doctrine. But, having thus declared his allegiance to a theory whose inadequacies the most orthodox Marxist-Leninists admit even as they justly proclaim its greatness, Sartre devotes hundreds and hundreds of pages to a dialectic of the *series* and the *group,* of consciousness and wholes, of the *practico-inert*[1] and *freedom,* which has nothing to do with Marxism, either that of Marx or that of the Marxist-Leninists, and which is itself ultimately difficult to reconcile with a properly historical dialectic. As long as scarcity lasts, human societies seem doomed to a static and seemingly eternal dialectic: alienation in the practico-inert; liberation, by action, of the group; the fatality of the organization of the group, then of institutions; and thus a relapse into the practico-inert. If humanity begins with revolt, it must endlessly repeat an enterprise which cannot succeed and which cannot be abandoned. (It is understandable that the Marxist-Leninists have not recognized their faith in this new myth of Sisyphus.)

The purely political debates recalled by the studies included in this book belong to the past. In one sense they are only of historical interest; they evoke the "crisis of conscience" experienced by great intellectuals in a country where the Communist

[1] For an explanation of this term, see p. 170.

party was too powerful for the left to be able to exclude it without thereby sacrificing its chances of arriving at power, and where the conservative parties and the government itself appeared for a certain period incapable of promoting social progress. In other countries this crisis of conscience does not yet belong to the past. The American reader, who will be inclined to regard these academic controversies as pointless and narrowly French, should not forget that they are being echoed throughout the Third World, at least in Latin America, and that these professors have disciples and rivals in many capitals, from Warsaw to Havana and Rio de Janeiro. Marxism and existentialism, sometimes separately and sometimes together, although often regarded as anachronistic by English or American philosophers committed to logical positivism or to the analysis of language, continue to represent one of the major philosophical tendencies of our age. This is why I continue to take seriously questions that were and still are raised by Marxists and existentialists. (Perhaps many of those who agree with my conclusions, especially in the United States, will criticize me for taking too seriously debates which do not merit so much attention or respect. I believe they would be wrong to react in this way, even if they are professionals in the field of philosophy. Frankly, linguistic analysis as it is practiced in many universities sometimes strikes me as just as pointless as the argument between Camus and Sartre about the relation between revolt and revolution, or the argument between Sartre and Merleau-Ponty about the relation between class and party, or between actual experience and action.) Although I have disagreed radically with Sartre, by education and interests, I belong to the same universe he does. It is by placing myself on the ground common to Marxism and existentialism that I am able to engage in discussion with friends of my youth, adversaries of yesterday, and colleagues of today. It is by using the same concepts and referring to the same values that I try to convince them of their errors.

What is this "common ground" of Marxism and existentialism? I would define it as *the calling into question of both the destiny of the individual and the historical destiny of mankind.* In the beginning, before 1940, Sartre pondered the destiny of the individual, and it seems to me that he has remained more a moralist than a sociologist. I do not think that *La Critique de la raison dialectique* reaches the same level as *L'Etre et le néant,* and I doubt whether Sartre succeeded in this last book in integrating the Marxist notion of the collective salvation of humanity by the proletarian revolution into a philosophy of solitary consciousness. But what concerns me here is not the success or failure of this "Marxianized existentialism" or this "existentialized Marxism," but the very fact of the conjunction, the link recognized between human condition and historical evolution. I recognize this link myself, and in this sense I would be tempted to acknowledge my debt to the Marxist *method,* insofar as this method combines an existential dimension (what is the lot that falls to man in a given regime?), a sociological dimension (what are the distinctive characteristics of a socio-economic regime?), and a historical dimension (what are the broad lines of development of modern society?). My anti-Marxism, as the reader of these essays will discover, has to do primarily with the rejection of the scheme of historical development elaborated by the Marxists on the basis of the Preface to *A Contribution to the Critique of Political Economy,* a scheme which can be supported only with the addition of so many complementary hypotheses that it is better, in accordance with the customary rules of science, simply to abandon it. It also has to do with the rejection of a philosophy or political position which can only be justified by an unknown future.

Within certain limits, justification by the future is inevitable and legitimate. Every political decision is a gamble that will be won or lost as a result of events which are beyond our control. The risk that the regime that comes out of a revolution may be worse than the existing regime is not sufficient reason to condemn revolutionaries. Action, like life itself, is always attended by risk. Under certain circumstances a man of feeling will prefer the risks of revolution, even a Communist revolution, to the intolerable vices of the established order. Let the American reader make no mistake: if I lived in the United States, I would probably devote more time to denouncing the anti-Communist obsession than I would to dispelling the illusions of "liberals" attracted by Marxism.

If justification by the future is inseparable from the historical condition of man, it always involves a danger which is moral as well as human. Although there is no politics without violence, the man of action is less reluctant to resort to violence when he sets himself a sublime goal. Mentally putting himself in the place of our grandchildren, he serenely declares that the sacrifices of today will have long been forgotten when men are reaping the benefits of established socialism. I plead for the living, not against those who will come after them, but against the casualness with which intellectuals of good will agree to let the living suffer for the possible profit of those who are not yet born. Let us not encourage an inevitable tendency of our civilization. Modern societies are and must be *futurist:* they claim to know in advance what they will be like, and technicians are inclined to be even more irritated by the resistance of men than by that of things.

What are the arguments in a defense of the living or an indictment of the abuses of justification by the future? I see three, proceeding from the least important to the most important, or from science to philosophy.

It is quite true that the future is not determined and that men, by their consciousness, by their will, help to shape it. But they have more chance of shaping a future that corresponds to their aspirations if they distinguish precisely what depends on them and what does not depend on them. But the Marxists—and the Marxian existentialists, following their example—assume as determined in advance what is incapable of being known and perhaps even of being realized. They subordinate freedom to a pseudo-fatality and enslave it to myths. The Marxist-Leninist, insofar as he adheres to the classical scheme of Marxism, assumes socialism to be the predetermined culmination of historical evolution. He transfigures socialism into the end of prehistory, he sees it as a radical break in the course of human events, an order incomparable to that of all known societies. Therefore all means, however horrible, are sanctified by the chosen and inevitable goal. Existentialists who do not succeed in breaking away from Marxist millenarism argue along similar lines but with more reservations: the goal is sublime, it makes it impossible to condemn the enterprise, but it is not enough to justify it completely. The *intellectual* error consists in foreseeing the regime (which, at a distance of a few dozen years, is difficult to do) instead of foreseeing merely the distinctive and universal traits of modernity which will be found in varying degrees in all industrially developed societies without this meaning that these societies must all choose the same regime; for an economic or political regime is merely one solution among others to the problem or problems which every economy or political regime must solve. In transferring the necessity and foreseeability of *regimes* to the *development* itself one does not devaluate conflicts between regimes, one does not substitute ironic dreams for warlike realities, one is armed against the snares and seductions of fanaticism.

Perhaps, in order to act and fight, many men need to assign an absolute value to a historical cause which is almost always uncertain and never entirely pure. Personally, at least in our time, I prefer to teach an active pessimism, though I am not unaware that a teaching of this kind disappoints many of the very persons who share my preferences. If the development is necessary and foreseeable rather than the regime, then an objective, systematic comparison of various economic, political, and social regimes becomes necessary. But this comparison will also serve as an antidote to the abuses of the justification by the future. If we observe class conflicts in various societies, if we study scarcity and the conditions that would allow us to overcome it, we shall have difficulty making reasonable sense out of notions like "the end of prehistory" or "homogeneous society." All regimes will be reduced to the same level, all parties will belong to the same species. We demand of collectives virtues which we do not assign to men as individuals.

How can we be astonished that no regime *simultaneously* satisfies all the values to which we are devoted, that each party has a clean conscience and is unaware of what it sacrifices?

The third argument, which is alone decisive in spite of its ambiguity, I feel strongly without being capable of expressing it precisely. What horrifies me about secular religions is the breakdown of the distinction between the profane and the sacred, between one class and the messiah, between one regime and the kingdom of God. Christians should feel this horror more strongly than I do, but in fact some of them, certain worker-priests for example, have, on the contrary, been attracted by the structural similarity of the opposing beliefs. I do not believe that man has any other destiny than on this earth and in this history. I am quite aware that religions, even those that address themselves to the individual soul and theoretically devaluate social hierarchies, have all at one time or another sanctioned and almost sanctified temporal hierarchies. Nevertheless I continue to regard religion as essentially the negation or at least the questioning of social values, which are always distributed among men according to criteria to which neither the reason nor the heart can fully subscribe. But the Marxists and the existentialists (at least Sartre and his followers), in their radical atheism, ultimately reduce existence to action; indeed, ultimately they place historical action above everything. Thus, in the last analysis, devotion to party becomes the highest merit and rebellion the "beginning of humanity." The human type of the militant is not without nobility. However, the revolutionary of today or of yesterday obeys a party which extends to a mission in the name of historical myths; he fights his fellow men with a view to eternal peace, but in the meantime he wages permanent war. With no other criterion than the truth of the party, with no other certitude than the rejection of the present, the militant, whether Marxist or existentialist, is in fact a nihilist.

Marxist nihilism is based on the conception of historical necessity. Sartrian nihilism is based on the conception of an empty freedom which, finding itself alienated in the real, can recover itself only in revolt. The alliance between a philosophy of historical determinism and a philosophy of individual freedom devoid of all determinacy and independent of any imperative may be fundamentally less paradoxical than it appears at first glance. The values of the first are derived from an alleged determinism; the values of the second arise from a pure freedom. Marxists and followers of Sartre do not reject the values of the humanist and rationalist tradition; if both groups are just as able to accept terror in the name of freedom, it is because by reducing man to action or by subordinating the individual to history, they have deprived themselves of the means of rejecting the unacceptable. Even Sartre, who denies all objective historical determinism, ends by admitting that socialism had *necessarily* to take the form of the "cult of personality." The philosopher of freedom is unable to condemn, even retrospectively, the crimes of Stalinism.

These critical studies may seem negative; they are above all a negation of the nihilism which is implicit in a certain kind of Marxism or a certain kind of existentialism. In this sense they have, in my opinion, a positive content. Their aim is to make man aware of the irreducible plurality of the dimensions that characterize his existence. They want to remind him of certain commonplace truths: political action is not the only form of action, revolution is not the only form of political action; submission to an alleged historical necessity may become the worst form of alienation. The fact that crimes may be forgotten by our grandchildren does not make them forgivable at the time they are committed. To substitute the future perfect for the simple future is too convenient. Ethics judges politics as much as politics judges ethics. Nobody can say in what circumstances one must prevail over the other, and everybody must decide this question for himself alone, at the risk of being mistaken. The worst error would be to fail to recognize this dialectic which determines our condition and to surrender totally to nihilism or fanaticism, either by denying all spiritual imperatives or by trusting blindly in an alleged determinism of history.

FIRST DIALOGUE
After the Liberation,
Before the Rupture

Sartre and the Marxist-Leninists

The dialogue between the existentialists and the Marxists, or more precisely, between Sartre and the Communists, has occupied the foreground of the French politico-literary scene since the liberation.

It is a strange dialogue, in which one of the voices declares its friendship and receives nothing but rebuffs in return. The existentialists have given repeated evidence of good will; Sartre, in an interview, went so far as to describe the differences between the Communists and himself as a family quarrel. The Communists have usually replied by declaring existentialism to be a petit-bourgeois ideology that has become progressively more reactionary and is on the way to becoming fascist.

Here are two examples of this Communist literature, one from *Pravda* and the other from a German newspaper. *Pravda* (January 23, 1947) writes:

The reactionary bourgeoisie protects Mr. Jean-Paul Sartre because it needs him in its struggle against democracy and against Marxism. The defeat of fascism destroyed the ideological defense of the two hundred families. It was necessary to find something new, and this is why an attempt is now being made to spread this mystical smoke screen which is existentialism over the French youth that is emerging from the harsh school of the resistance. . . .

. . . The weekly magazine *Life* published a laudatory biography of Mr. Sartre which stressed the fact that on the ideological level, this young philosopher was the principal enemy of Marxism today. This means that the writings of Mr. Sartre, as well as those of the

Maison Paquin, are assured of being imported into the United States. And Mr. Sartre knows what is required of him. Shortly after his return from the United States, Mr. Sartre published a special issue devoted to the United States. This time the plague-spreaders wanted to be serious: they concerned themselves with economic problems and with the most important of these, that of currency. Mr. Sartre himself speaks of Americanism only with condescension. But the article next to it, by Mr. Guy Cardailhac, gives the solution to the Sartrian philosophy. It explains that the entire world constitutes the heritage of the United States; that whether France likes it or not, she must allow herself to be led by America, must join a Western or Atlantic bloc—in plain language, must become a colony of American imperialism. Here we see the economic and social aspect of existentialism. The plague-spreaders like to talk about death, but they want to live, and to live well off the fruit of their pens. For them, American reaction is a commercial center, an outlet, and they in turn are necessary to the rich American bourgeoisie, since they are the enemies of Marxism.

The passage from the *Tägliche Rundschau* is even more violent. It is by the German writer Niekisch, who once belonged to the National Socialist party, or at least to what constituted its extreme left. As such he had been denounced by the Nazi party in 1934, if memory serves me correctly, and he concludes a long article as follows:

If with Kierkegaard and Nietzsche existentialism remains within the limits of a great and serious philosophy, with Sartre it becomes a cynical and frivolous game of all or nothing.

It is no accident that Sartre is finally purveying his existentialism in novels and plays and that he is exploiting it commercially in the theater.

We still remember how delightedly Hitler talked about "decadence" and a "decadent age." In reducing existentialism to a philosophy of frivolous adventure and risk, of cynical flirtation with the weariness of existence, he was merely expressing what a fascist era was feeling, thinking, and doing. If you note what kinds of people gather around Sartre, you will understand exactly why Heidegger was catapulted to such honors in France. The existentialism which in Kierkegaard had a sublime and moving aspect has degenerated until today it is no more than the nauseating odor of decomposition enveloping a social order which is at its last gasp and is suffering the throes of the death agony.

Idiocies of this kind, uninteresting as they are in themselves, have a symbolic value, and they will provide me with a point of departure from which to define one of the questions I should like to raise.

When existentialism offers itself to Marxism as a possible philosophical foundation, is it right or wrong? Can it be carried all the way? Can it provide a philosophy of Communism? Or is Marxism right in rejecting existentialism? Obviously, I shall not examine the question on the political level, the level of passages I have quoted above, but on the philosophical level.

If we refer to the philosophical writings of Sartre and Merleau-Ponty, the question arises in approximately these terms (at least, they raise it in these terms): We are in agreement, they say, with the revolutionary aim of Marxism, we accept its inspiration and its desire, but Marxism also takes the form of a materialism which is self-contradictory and inconceivable, and we cannot accept a doctrine which would oblige us to dismiss reason. Existentialism is the true philosophy of revolution, and if the Marxists yielded to our philosophical arguments there would be nothing left to divide us.

I should like, therefore, first to review the principal points of Sartre's critique of materialism, and next to show how existentialism offers itself to Marxism as the philosophy capable of providing its foundation.

On the critique of materialism I shall be brief, because these are classic ideas and because Sartre attacks interpreters of Marxism such as Roger Garaudy, whose ideological docility is more evident than his philosophical validity. The principal themes of Sartre's critique of materialism seem to be approximately as follows:

1. It is impossible to explain consciousness as an object among other objects, as popular materialism does. Every ex-

planation of consciousness in terms of something outside of it is contradictory, because the explanation already presupposes the very thing it claims to explain. If consciousness is regarded as an object among other objects, thought is reduced to a reflection or an effect, and it is impossible to understand how one fragmentary object "gets unstuck" from the world of objects, how it ever succeeds in reflecting the totality of objects or in grasping a truth. Thus we arrive at a first proposition: materialism, which would offer itself as a denial of consciousness or a total explanation of the determination of consciousness, refutes itself. It is impossible not to assume the *cogito* or subjectivity from the outset.

2. Current accounts of Marxist materialism reveal a constant and almost hopeless confusion of scientism or positivism, rationalism, and materialism. Marxist materialists declare that they reject all metaphysics and that they simply take the results of science as such; but the results of science by themselves do not and never will demonstrate materialism. The statement that there is only one reality which is material reality is essentially metaphysical, and goes just as far beyond the results of science as the statements of idealism. If, on the other hand, one abides by the results of science purely and simply, if one refuses to go beyond them, one has no business proclaiming the essential rationality of nature or history. Thus the Marxist-Leninists either combine the three theses—positivist, materialist, and rationalist—or pass confusedly from one to the other: the positivist thesis, that we must accept the sciences as they are, group them and organize them; the metaphysical thesis, the statement that only matter exists or that the external world exists as we see it or as science analyzes it; and the thesis of the intrinsic rationality of the object, which the Marxists try to retain, although they have eliminated its foundations.

3. The third argument is probably the most important. There is a contradiction between the two notions of materialism and of the dialectic. Sartre frequently returns to this point.

He begins by assuming a radical difference between the

purely external relations of objects in space or, generally speaking, relations of spatial externality, and the dialectical movement. The latter is by nature a movement of ideas: it implies synthesis and totality, a further stage which at once surpasses and preserves the previous state, a kind of appeal of the future or a tendency of totality to realize itself. The dialectic, thus defined, appears as immediately irreconcilable with the order of spatial and material relations to which some would reduce it. As an example of this antinomy Sartre takes the case of the ideological superstructure, and shows how, in materialist explanations, a transition is made from a simple determinist explanation—the idea is the effect or reflection of a certain material situation—to an explanation which would lead to the dialectic: the idea arises in a historical situation to respond to needs or to go beyond a given state toward a state to be created.

If the two movements—the movement of spatial relations and the movement of creative or dialectic progression—are incompatible, then the introduction of the dialectical movement into matter betrays a confused or contradictory notion of matter. The Marxists claim that by beginning with the simplest matter one rises to the complex forms of reality: inorganic nature, life, the world of history, mind. A hierarchy of this kind is certainly not incomprehensible, but if one adheres to the conception of crude matter, how is one to explain the progression from the inferior to the superior type, unless one has begun with a contradictory notion of matter, surreptitiously introducing the superior terms into the initial term?

These, rapidly summarized, are the three essential points of Sartre's critique of Marxist materialism. These are the arguments by which he tries to justify his refusal to adopt an absurd doctrine.

Once materialism has been ruled out, Sartre concedes that the doctrine is certainly no intellectual whim. The revolutionaries supported the materialist ideology or myth for serious reasons, but, asks Sartre, cannot the needs which materialism answers be satisfied, and satisfied much better, by existentialism? This brings us to the second part of the dialogue between Sartre and the Marxists, or rather the monologue of Sartre. Here are the positive offers, as it were, which he addresses to them; here is how existentialism could be the philosophy of revolution. Here again, I shall try to select the essential ideas.

1. The conception of man or thought "in situation" is the perfect solution to the necessities of revolution. In effect, to say that man or thought is "in situation" is to say that in a single and identical movement, consciousness sees through the reality existing around it and goes beyond it. Man is "in situation," but this situation is not an absolute: he becomes "unstuck" from the context into which he is inserted and he manages to achieve an over-all view of it precisely because he wants to go beyond it. But this knowledge of the existing totality by man in "situation" is precisely what the revolutionary needs and what materialism claimed to provide. In fact, materialism claimed to give the revolutionary a thought which at the same time knows the world and wants to transform it; but this double relation of knowledge and transformation is also provided, and indeed, more effectively provided, by "thought in situation," the typical formula of existentialism.

2. Materialism had one essential virtue for the revolutionaries: it provided an escape from the mystifications of the upper classes. The man of the privileged classes—this is still Sartre speaking, and I am summarizing or paraphrasing—is, by nature, a man who assumes certain rights, who claims not to be a purely natural man, a man like others, who automatically arrogates to himself certain prerogatives or privileges. An essential function of materialism, in revolutionary thought, is to explain this would-be superior by the inferior, to bring the man who has rights down to the level of ordinary men, to bring the man who enjoys a metaphysical rank, as it were, down to the level of natural man. But, adds Sartre, existentialism offers the same virtues: indeed, according to this doctrine, man is purely contingent, he is "thrown there" without knowing why, without reason or immediate purpose. By arriving at this existential consciousness, man will no longer be the victim of the mystifications of the upper classes. Just as well as and even better than

the materialist, the existentialist will explain that these rights to which the privileged classes tend to give a metaphysical substance are merely the expression of a social situation. Existentialism will demonstrate the historicity of values as such, and in so doing it will make it possible to go beyond them.

3. The function or purpose of materialism is to give the worker a consciousness of determinism. More precisely, according to Sartre, the worker, in his contact with nature, discovers determinism, discovers the force of the links which bind things together. Because he is in contact with nature, he escapes the bourgeois world of civility and recognizes the rude necessity of things. This determinism is real, and it is true that the worker discovers it in work, but it is not total. On the contrary, determinism will better meet the needs of a revolutionary doctrine if it is fixed within limits. This makes it possible to determine the effect of a given act and leaves the possibility of transforming the over-all reality to man; it reveals the law of his action and the conditions of effectiveness, but it safeguards the consciousness of freedom, the consciousness of being able to change the existing order of things. Thus, here again existentialism, correctly interpreted, offers to a greater degree and better than classical materialism a partial determinism which is dominated and enhanced by freedom.

4. Thanks to materialism, history no longer occurs in the empyrean of ideas. Life itself and the struggle gradually bring about the realization of human ends. Similarly, existentialism, in essence, assumes both man acting and the resistance of objects; it analyzes the dialectic of man and obstacles; here again, it provides everything that materialism could want and demand.

In short, certain existentialist ideas are proposed as a philosophical foundation for a revolutionary aim: the recognition and the reflexive primacy of subjectivity, the fact that consciousness is perpetually unsatisfied and in a single movement discovers reality and wants to transcend it; thought is "in situation," contingent man has no *raison d'être*, but is simply "there," values are historical, man is free. The Sartrian doctrine could serve as a basis for a revolutionary aim because it assumes freedom as a metaphysical *donnée* without robbing the impulse of liberation of significance; freedom as such is never completely eliminated, but is always in danger of being violated or curtailed.

Merleau-Ponty went even further in the attempt to argue from existentialist themes to Marxist themes. Referring quite rightly to the youthful writings of Marx, he showed that a number of the themes of existentialism were already present in these writings. Here again I shall summarize, isolating a few ideas which seem to be the meeting points of the existentialists and the Marxists.

Existentialism goes beyond both materialism and idealism, as does Marxism. I shall quote only one passage, from the *Economic and Philosophic Manuscripts:* "We see here that naturalism or realized humanism differs from idealism as well as from materialism, and is at the same time the truth which unites them both. At the same time we see that only naturalism is capable of comprehending universal history."

When existentialism refuses to be materialist and claims to go beyond this classic antinomy it is merely following the initial movement of Marxist thought. Moreover, what is at the foundation, the origin of the Marxist conception of history, is not matter at all; it is man in action. The bearer of history is not some indefinable matter, it is concrete man, body and soul, in contact with nature and creating, through work, his conditions of existence. By beginning with this conception of concrete man it is possible to give a more reasonable and more satisfying interpretation of Marxist formulas which become almost incomprehensible in the popular versions—for example, the relation between infrastructure and superstructure, the alleged determination of ideas, which are thus reduced to mere reflections, by the material foundation. These formulas are actually rather difficult to understand in a rigorous manner. On the other hand, if man is seen *primarily* in relation to nature and if this relation involves a certain form of appropriation of natural forces, then it is possible to understand all the activities of an individual or a group in terms of this original attitude and this fundamental impulse. It is no longer a question of the

exclusive determination of the other sectors by the primary
sector; each sector is understood in and by the whole.

Moreover, by beginning with this same definition of concrete man, bearer of history, one could arrive at a new interpretation of the relation between the individual and society
and discover the dialectic of the individual and circumstances.

In the Marxist vision of history, circumstances are the result
of human acts which each generation finds as if hardened or
crystalized around it. It is important never to regard these circumstances as final, definitive, or fixed once and for all, but on
the contrary, to remember always that their existence is inseparable from human behavior. This is the dialectic between the
individual and society; man, by his activity, creates an order
of external relations which appear to his descendents as a
destiny; but in reality a situation is never definitive, it is always
being remade both by the gaze which contemplates it and by
the will which transcends it.

One could also show a kind of analogy or spiritual affinity
between the Marxist critique of ideologies and the existentialist
effort to arrive at the fundamental human attitude. One of the
objectives of Marxist thought was to criticize and expose the
alienations, the projections of both ideas and acts which, although products of man, elude their creator, and beyond this
critique, to reach the essential reality of living man as defined
by his relations with nature and other men. Similarly, there is
in existentialism a desire to expose the ideological fictions
which imprison our minds and to return, beyond bad faith, to
the choice which man authentically makes of himself.

The tendency, which I believe is common to Sartre and
Merleau-Ponty, is to define an existentialist anthropology,
whose broad lines I have tried to trace, which may also be considered if not Marxist according to Leninist or Stalinist orthodoxy, at least capable of serving as a foundation for the revolutionary philosophy of Marxism.

These arguments of existentialism cannot be said to have
elicited an equally coherent answer on the part of the Marxists.
The answers vary according to the intelligence of the speakers,

and the answers of Henri Lefebvre are certainly more perti-
nent and more interesting than those of Roger Garaudy. I
do not intend to analyze them in detail, precisely because they
do not constitute a logical whole; all I wish to do in the second
part of this article is explain, on the level of ideology or psychology, why the Marxists are reluctant to accept the existentialist propositions. Next, I should like to show why it is fundamentally impossible to call oneself an existentialist and a
Marxist at the same time—why these two philosophies are incompatible in their intentions, their origins, and their ultimate
ends.

What are the psychological or ideological reasons why official theorists do not accept the version of Marxism which the
existentialists have offered them? A first reason seems to be the
enormous prestige of science, the regret which the Marxists
would feel in no longer calling themselves scientific, in re-
linquishing their claim to scientific truth as such. In the United
States, as in Russia, there persists a nineteenth-century philosophy of progress in the strict sense of the term: an absolute confidence in science as a transforming force directed toward the
well-being of human societies. It seems to me that science still
enjoys enormous prestige among all Marxists; but in the interpretation of Marxism which existentialists give, Marxism is no
longer a scientific truth.

For my own part, I consider it absurd to attribute a truth of
a scientific, positive order to the Marxist philosophy of history.
There is no common measure between the theory that social
contradictions lead spontaneously to a classless society and a
mathematical or physical proposition. When Marx contrasted
scientific socialism with utopian socialism, he was thinking of
two ways of approaching social problems; utopian socialism, in
his eyes, was a form of socialism which first established an end
and next tried to determine the means of attaining this end,
whereas socialism is scientific when it is content to determine
the development of history; but a scientific socialism according
to which reality itself, by its own spontaneous movement, tends
to realize the ideal is not a science in the sense of a natural,

mathematical, or physical science. The Marxists—and I understand them, at least from a pragmatic point of view—are afraid to formulate these distinctions explicitly: for once you admit that the truth of Marxism, if truth there be, is of a philosophical rather than a scientific nature, the parties which call themselves Marxist lose the certainty of victory along with the prestige of science.

If, moreover, you were to accept this philosophically more complex and more subtle version of Marxism, you would encounter difficulties on two essential points: first, the *necessary* movement by which the classless society is to be achieved through the contradictions of present society; and second, the relation between the material infrastructure and the totality of political and ideological superstructures. Indeed, in an allegedly scientific version of Marxism, the realization of the classless society is *necessary*, given the contradictions of capitalism, and at the same time significant. In other words, the same movement is at once necessary, in the sense of determinism, and historically rational: it corresponds to the meaning of history, and it is inevitable. If one adopts a philosophical version of Marxism, one must, as I shall try to show a little later, make a distinction between the real or alleged determinism which leads to the socialist goal and the significance of this goal: socialism may be necessary rationally without being necessary on the level of determinism (socialism or barbarism). The coincidence of the two can be assumed only in a scientistic mythology.

In the second place, when the relation of infrastructure to superstructure is interpreted strictly, in the sense of determination or reflection, the result is a simplification of political practice; one may regard as essential and sufficient the realization of the material foundation of socialism, or socialization of the means of production. If, on the contrary, one maintains a philosophically more subtle interpretation of the relation between infrastructure and superstructure, one will be closer to the truth, but the socialization of the means of production will no longer rule out all varieties of conflict or alienation, and consequently, it will be less easy to justify what will happen after the revolution. In other words, in accepting a total determinism of a scientific order, one simplifies at once the determination of the goal of socialism, the movement toward this goal, and the relation between the material base and the superstructure.

Finally, although the existentialist may insist that he is just as much of a revolutionary as the Communist, he cannot eliminate a fundamental difference: when one reads *L'Etre et le néant,* one breathes a Pascalian atmosphere. The essential theme of philosophy is the relation of the solitary individual either to God or to the absence of God. (In the case of Sartre, it is the dialogue of the solitary man with the absence of God.) If this dialogue is the essence of the human condition, men must inevitably be diverted from what, in the eyes of the Marxist, is of primary importance, namely revolution. I do not go so far as to say that there is an incompatibility between the Pascalian anguish and the revolutionary impulse. To regard the revolutionary problem as one of the human problems is not to eliminate that of Pascal; but the revolutionary, being concerned only with that which leads to revolution, will feel differently about it. To reinterpret Marxism in terms of a dialogue of the individual with God or with nothingness is to distract man from the urgent task and consequently to weaken the force of the Marxist doctrine.

Up to this point I have developed these reasons for the Marxist rejection on the level of ideology or psychology. I will now try to show that they may be justified in a more rigorously philosophical manner, and that actually existentialism can never be carried as far as Marxism—that is, of course, without ceasing to be existentialist. In other words, if one remains an existentialist one will never be a Marxist.

A follower of Kierkegaard cannot at the same time be a follower of Marx. If, as Marxism claims, revolution provides the solution to the philosophical problems, one cannot at the same time assume a dialectic, by definition incomplete, between the lone individual and God or nothingness. I shall return to this essential point a little further on.

Let us begin with the elements common to existentialism and Marxism. I really believe that these elements—thought in situation, discovery and transcendence, unsatisfied consciousness, the historicity of values—belong to Marxism as well as to existentialism. After all, these ideas are really nothing but the more or less formalized residuum of an anthropology derived from Hegel. There can be no doubt that existentialism and Marxism have a common origin in a philosophy of a Hegelian type. Sartre and Merleau-Ponty emphasize certain aspects of the human condition. But to argue from this formal anthropology to a Marxist anthropology it is necessary to bring in other ideas, of which some might conceivably be assimilated by existentialism (although they have not belonged to it up to now), and others could never find a place in existentialism, at least not in that version of existentialism set forth in *L'Etre et le néant*.

The fact is that in order to arrive at a Marxist anthropology it is not enough to say that man is "in situation" or even that the bearer of history is concrete man; one must assume as a first proposition, commonplace but fundamental, that work is the essence of man, or that the relation of man to nature, a relation by which he learns to master natural forces and at the same time creates his own living conditions, is the decisive relation. Is this definition of man in terms of the struggle with nature existentialist or not? The point is debatable; but there is no doubt that strictly speaking, the idea of work as the essence of man plays no role in the existentialism of Sartre. This idea might conceivably be added to it, although I think it gives the doctrine an entirely different slant from that of *L'Etre et le néant*.

From the fact that man is defined essentially by his relation to nature or the mode of appropriation of natural forces, Marx goes on to an explanation of relations among men. The relations of men to one another, that is, above all their struggle, is present in Sartre as it is in Marx, but when one reads *L'Etre et le néant* one has the impression that the struggle of conscious individuals among themselves is eternal, given as such once and for all. This raises the essential question. Either this struggle of conscious beings among themselves is a permanent quality of the human condition which could not conceivably be transcended, or else the struggle of conscious beings among themselves occurs within history, of which it is the moving force. To put it differently, either man's consciousness is confined within the dialectic of *L'Etre et le néant,* or the true dialectic of consciousness is one which unfolds in history, and it is creative. To be sure, it is not impossible to begin with existentialism and then reintroduce the idea that the struggle of conscious beings among themselves, occurring through history, creates the works and regimes of civilization. However, *L'Etre et le néant* does not suggest that history is a creative process by which through struggle—with nature and among themselves—men arrive at liberty and consequently transcend the contradictions. The impression is rather that "eternally each conscious being wishes the death of the other."

But to move from existentialism to Marxism, the dialectic of the solitary individual must become a dialectic that is properly historical, history must be the true history of human consciousness; it is necessary, therefore, that history have a meaning, a progressive and creative meaning. If we consider not, perhaps, the writings of Sartre himself, but a novel by Simone de Beauvoir, history is reduced to a series of failures. In the writings of the existentialists the accent is placed much more on the essential and inevitable character of failure in all human enterprises than on the idea of a creative dialectic or the possibility of reconciliation.

Even supposing it were possible to incorporate into existentialism the idea that the struggles of men have a meaning, that the progression of social regimes has a meaning, that we do not witness the indefinite repetition of the same vain enterprise, in order to be a Marxist it is further necessary to arrive at a final solution, it is necessary that history ultimately realize philosophy. Everyone knows the famous statement of Marx, "One can triumph over philosophy only by realizing it." Man will cease to be a prisoner of philosophical abstraction only by creating within the social reality itself a situation consistent

with the idea of the human vocation which philosophy has provided. History must provide the solution to the philosophical
problem by revolution.

"This communism is, insofar as it is complete naturalism,
humanism, and insofar as it is complete humanism, naturalism;
it is the true solution to the struggle between origin and being,
between objectivity and subjectivity, between freedom and necessity, between the individual and the species. It is none other
than the solved enigma of history which reveals itself as being
this solution."

The young Marx was convinced—and he never changed his
mind—that revolution is not merely a political, economic, and
social accident. Revolution has a philosophical significance, it
is the realization of philosophy, it solves the enigma of history.
But I really wonder how Sartrism could ever regard the Communist revolution as the solution to the dialectic of *L'Etre et
le néant*. Obviously, it is permissible to favor the Communist
revolution for a particular political or economic reason, but
one could annex the doctrine of revolution as solution to the
philosophical problem only by inverting the basic assumptions
of *L'Etre et le néant*. An opposition of this kind is of decisive
importance, for in every philosophy of history or in every
political philosophy the greatest problem is to determine the
end.

The determination of the end is already difficult in the
Marxism of Marx, but it becomes more difficult and almost impossible in an existential version of Marxism. How did the
young Marx come to the conclusion that revolution is the solution to the philosophical problem? If we refer to the *Introduction to Hegel's Critique of the Philosophy of Law*, we shall find
a few fundamental themes which provide the answer to this
question. The two principal themes are the unity of the particular and the universal as expounded by Hegel, and the doctrine
of alienation in the *Economic and Philosophic Manuscripts*.

Marx does not so much criticize the actual idea of the state
that Hegel arrived at as show that this idea is not actually embodied in present society. Hegel observes, on the one hand, the

individual of "civil society," the individual of the political economy, the particular being who is the prisoner of his needs, his appetites and his selfish interests, and, on the other hand, the political man, the man who participates in the universality of the state. But in the eyes of Marx there is no unity between this particular man of concrete life and the man as citizen who dwells in the empyrean of ideas and whose participation in the state is not embodied in concrete life.

What is the significance of these abstract formulas? Man who works is trapped within his particularity: he is bound to another particular man, the one to whom he rents his labor force; he does not participate in the universal, he is not united with the collectivity. To be sure, as a citizen, an abstract political subject, he participates in the state, but this participation remains alien to his professional life. The Marxist revolution wants to abolish this duality between particularity isolated within itself and fictitious universality; it aims to abolish this alienation, to have the concrete individual live and work by participating directly in universality, which presupposes a revolution and the socialization of the means of production. The individual ceases to work for other individuals and works for the universality of the state. This is what determines the end of history, according to Marxism. This determination of the end assumes that Marx retained the whole of Hegel's system of thought and that he was trying to translate Hegel's idea into reality.

In other words, one analyzes history in terms of a certain doctrine of man and of the state, and one looks to history for a way of putting this doctrine into effect. It is on the basis of this true doctrine that the true end of human history is determined.

The other theme, that of alienation, leads us to analogous conclusions. In present society man is perpetually divided from himself, he is never in possession either of his capacities or his works, which elude him. The worker who sees the product of his labor belong to others is alienated, as is the entrepreneur who sees the products that he places on the market carried away by the anonymous movement of economic forces which nobody controls. One of Marx's essential ideas is the end of alienation: man must accomplish in himself the whole of his creations. The culmination is to be total man, who would actually enjoy the wealth that he has created for himself throughout history. Here again, it is in terms of a philosophical idea that history is considered and that its meaning is discovered.

Let us consider the case of the proletariat. The mission of the proletariat in history is by no means implicit in the situation of the proletarian. Marx, like Lenin, explained that the worker would not by himself discover the revolutionary truth: it is the intellectual, the philosopher, who reveal, to the proletariat the historic role which it is to assume. The proletarian, less and less bound to local conditions, will become universal man. He will be the representative par excellence of the alienation of human society. Because he will be stripped of everything, because he will be generic man, he will be the agent of universal history, destined to bring about its end. But this mission of the proletariat is comprehensible only through the knowledge of philosophy—Hegelian or Marxist philosophy —which, by discovering the overall meaning of history, can and must reveal it to the proletariat.

A Marxist conception of this kind involves two principal difficulties. On the one hand, this conception of history is based on the rational necessity of Communism. But the fact that the advent of Communism is necessary to realize the true idea of man and history does not yet imply that this advent is necessary in the sense of inevitable. The best proof of this is that sometimes the Marxists say: Communism or barbarism. Since there is an alternative, there may be a rational necessity for revolution from a philosophical point of view, but no causal necessity. On the other hand, in a philosophy of the Hegelian type, the truth normally reaches consciousness only after its realization. The true philosophy is the philosophy of the past. A philosophy in which the truth of the system coincides with that of history presupposes a completion of history on the basis of which the truth of the whole past is comprehended. Marxism wants to maintain for its chosen goal, that is, for a future that is nevertheless free, the prestige of absolute truth, of that total rational truth which should be reserved for a completed history. How is one to expound a true and total philosophy of history before that history is complete?

These two difficulties—the difficulty involving the lack of connection between rational necessity and causal necessity and the one involving the attribution of total truth to a history to come—are multiplied when one approaches the problems of history from the viewpoint of existentialism, that is, simply on the basis of a formal anthropology without a theory either of the society or of the state. Certainly Merleau-Ponty has tried to determine a meaning of history in history without resorting to system or doctrine as in Marxism, but it seems to me that he always confuses two ideas: the idea that history has a meaning and the idea that the meaning the Marxist assigns to it is the only valid, the only rationally admissible one. Man in history supposedly has the possibility of determining a meaning, a meaning universally valid, imperative for all. Merleau-Ponty has indicated several criteria for this meaning of history: socialization of the means of production, the growing initiative of the proletariat, and the tendency toward internationalism. But a glance at the present reality is enough to show that the three criteria do not go hand in hand: a given event may satisfy one and not another. In any case, there remains a fundamental difference between a point of view of this kind and the Marxist point of view.

Like a true intellectual, Merleau-Ponty wants the worker to be the true revolutionary: only the worker, having experienced oppression, would really want to abolish it. The Marxist, on the other hand, Marx as well as Lenin, holds that the worker alone, without the intellectual, can never determine the meaning of his mission. Left to himself, he will go no further than trade unionism. For him to become truly revolutionary, according to Lenin, there must be professional revolutionaries, revolutionary philosophers who will make the workers understand that the essential thing is not this or that partial improvement of their lot, but a desire for overall change. The philosophers will convince the proletariat that it alone is capable of this change, which will be the realization of philosophy. Existentialism, on the other hand, having no philosophy to realize, tries to recognize the valid meaning of history by starting with an experience of oppression or an experience of the situation of the working class in society. It seems to me that this solution is no more Marxist than it is satisfactory.

Anyone who wants to support the proletariat will belong in France to the Communist party and in England to the Labour party. It would be impossible to determine a historical end by referring solely to the proletariat and its alleged experience. On this point one must be more of a Marxist and recognize that it is a philosophical doctrine that leads one to the meaning of history. The necessary condition for determining a meaning of history that is universally valid is that the revolution not be an accident among others, but a solution to the philosophical problem. This brings me back to my fundamental theme. What will always prevent an existentialist from being a Marxist is that revolution will not solve his philosophical problem, that of the dialogue of the individual with the absence of God in atheist existentialism, and with God in the existentialism of the believer. Outside of this dialogue one may take an interest in the lot of the unfortunate and join the revolutionary party for some perfectly valid reason, but one will never arrive at the equivalent of a Marxist philosophy.

I am afraid that this argument is at bottom quite commonplace and somehow obvious. Merleau-Ponty has written, "At a certain point, the 'no' of Kierkegaard coincides with or approaches the 'no' of Marx to Hegel." There is, however, a radical difference between the two. When you begin with the *no* of Kierkegaard, you may arrive at Sartre, but never at Marxism. One cannot be at the same time the heir of Hegel–Marx and the heir of Kierkegaard.

It seems to me very understandable, therefore, that the Marxists, and the Communists in particular, reject existentialism. The Marxists may very well accept certain of Sartre's analyses of worry or anxiety, but they will accord them a very

different importance. Since consciousness is created and fulfilled in history, the description or dialectic of the fundamental
emotions, of anxiety, can never constitute the essential element
of ontology.

The reader will certainly have noticed to what a degree this
dialogue is strictly philosophical and metaphysical. The existentialists demand the renunciation of materialism; the Marxists
reply that one must choose between Kierkegaard and Marx, between the bourgeoisie and the proletariat. But about the historical situation in which both existentialists and Marxists are
living, nothing is said. The existentialists declare themselves
to be in agreement with the revolutionaries, but the reasons
they give are singularly abstract. They invoke Revolution for
its own sake, with a certain romantic resonance. But the existentialists, unlike the Marxists, are not supposed to know Revolution, but only revolutions. Sartre states, "The mind is on
the side of the proletariat," but in what sense does his philosophy justify a statement of this kind? Existentialism presents itself as a revolutionary doctrine, but it leaves the particular
content, the nature of this revolution in a limbo more suited
to rhetoric than to action. Actually, I think it is rather easy to
indicate why the existentialists fail to define the concrete significance of the revolution which they profess to desire.

Since 1848 and the youthful writings of Marx, history has
advanced, new facts have appeared. Marxism as a revolutionary
impulse, a movement to end alienation or to go beyond present
capitalist society, cannot be refuted by these facts. On the other
hand, these facts make it necessary to refine the historical
schema by which Marx explained the transition from capitalism
to socialism. This schema involved aggravation of the capitalist
contradictions, a progressive increase in the number of proletarians, and pauperization. A certain parallelism was assumed
between the contradictions of capitalism, the development of
the proletariat, and the chance of revolution.

The real evolution was quite different. The expansion of
capitalism did not bring about a pauperization of the working

class, but a rise in its standard of living. In the United States, the most capitalistic country today, the working class has the highest standard of living and the least desire for revolution. The only country where a revolution calling itself Marxist has succeeded is one where the objective conditions prescribed by Marxist doctrine were not given. This would suggest that revolution, even when it claims to be Marxist, is often a political phenomenon rather than the result of a gradual ripening of economic contradictions. Finally, the revolution having taken place in a single country, the post-capitalist regime has been associated with a historically singular society in which neither the state nor inequality has disappeared with revolution. The result is a situation which may not be contrary to Marxist doctrine, but which at least was not foreseen by it, in which the opposite terms are, on the one hand, a regime calling itself post-capitalist but established in a poor country, and, on the other hand, a capitalist regime in a rich country.

This opposition of wealth and Communism represents a fundamental difficulty in the most orthodox Marxism, and as proof I shall cite a very well-known passage in which Marx explains that revolution is not possible without sufficient development of the forces of production.

"Moreover, this development of the productive forces (which already implies that the present empirical existence of men unfolds *on the level of world history* rather than on the level of local life), is an absolutely indispensable practical prerequisite, for without it *poverty* would become general, and with *need*, the struggle for survival would begin again, and all would inevitably fall back into the same ancient mire."

My thesis is that in the country where the revolution took place the people fell back into the "ancient mire," in the Marxist sense of the term. But surely if one wants to reconsider Marxism today, it is not enough to expound about the concept of matter or alienation; one should analyze the present situation with its paradoxical character in relation to Marx's expectations. Marxists and Communists as well as existentialists seem, in their dialogue, to be somewhat indifferent to the problems which I have just suggested and which nevertheless strike me as essential. These problems do not have merely a political and practical significance, they force one to reconsider certain philosophical themes of Marxism, like that of the overcoming of alienation or post-capitalist society.

Why does neither group seem disposed to analyze or interpret this paradoxical historical situation? With the existentialists, this resistance has to do with the ambiguity of their position. They wish to be revolutionaries, and in France at least, where the only revolutionary party is the Communist party, their sympathies lie on that side. On the other hand, for many reasons, they cannot or will not embrace Communism. Consequently they often invoke the philosophical inadequacies of popular Marxism to justify their refusal. I think there are many other reasons, and I am afraid that the ambiguity which is so striking in the political attitude of the existentialists results not merely from the philosophical conflicts between Marxism and existentialism, which I have tried to indicate, but from a certain difficulty in confronting the present situation. I always have the impression that existentialism, while invoking commitment, seldom succeeds in committing itself; that it experiences extreme difficulty in adopting a concrete historical and political attitude. I shall not be betraying a confidence when I say that in the days when there was a board of editors on the review *Les Temps modernes,* one day one of its members expressed the desire to impose on all of us the obligation not to belong to any party. This consequence of a philosophy of commitment seemed to me rather surprising.

As far as the Marxists are concerned, their recourse to the materialist myth does not seem to be inspired only by the reasons which Sartre gives. The materialist myth implies a historical determinism which would *necessarily* lead to the regime of the classless society. One imagines a historical necessity which would of itself realize the meaning of history. In a period like ours it is convenient to possess a determinism consistent with the meaning of history. Otherwise one would come up against great difficulties and would be obliged at least to examine the different attitudes possible in terms of traditional Marxism. The first is that of Stalinism, which regards present Russian society as one stage on the road to the realization of the classless society. The second is the Trotskyist attitude, according to which the road that leads to the classless society does not pass through the Soviet regime, but requires a new revolutionary movement of the international proletariat. Finally, one would have to argue with those who maintain that the realization of post-capitalist society by means of the seizure of power by a single party which assumed absolute authority, far from promoting human liberation by the socialization of the means of production, leads to a tyranny worse than that of capitalism. Thus there would be a third possible attitude, also Marxist, which I shall call *progressisme,* and which would try to realize progressively, without the seizure of power by violence or the dictatorship of a single party, the material and beyond that, the spiritual ends of traditional Marxism.

These last brief remarks are merely intended to suggest that the discussion between existentialism and Marxism is richer in metaphysical controversy than it is in concrete study of the situation of France or the world, perhaps because neither group wants to see the original elements of this situation or to assume responsibility for it.

SECOND DIALOGUE
After Stalin,
Before the Twentieth Congress

The Adventures and
Misadventures of Dialectics*

The originality of Maurice Merleau-Ponty's latest book, like the one that preceded it, is that it combines philosophy and politics.

Beginning with the Moscow trials, *Humanisme et Terreur* had analyzed the problem of action in history, the ambiguity of the condition of man, who is at once innocent and guilty. The Soviet Union did not represent one economic and social regime among others, one attempt at accelerated industrialization in a country of non-Western traditions influenced by the West: it embodied the hopes of humanity. With Lenin, Trotsky, and Stalin, Historical Reason was playing its last card. *Les Aventures de la dialectique* falls within the same line of thought, but comes to an opposite conclusion. In 1948, philosophy served to demonstrate that the Soviet experiment was more than itself since it was a decisive moment in the historical dialectic. In 1955, philosophy suggests that the Communist experiment is nothing more than itself; whether this experiment succeeds or fails, Historical Reason will not be affected.

Although the mixture of philosophy and politics gives very different results in 1948 and in 1955, the two books have a

---

* In 1955 Maurice Merleau-Ponty published *Les Aventures de la dialectique*, in which he criticized the positions taken by Sartre in a series of articles in *Les Temps modernes* entitled *Les Communistes et la paix*. In that same year I published *L'Opium des intellectuels*. The two articles which follow were written at the end of 1955 and appeared in the review *Preuves* early in 1956.

unique characteristic: in both, philosophical arguments are dominant. Indeed, by a kind of paradox, *Les Aventures de la dialectique,* which concludes with the necessity of knowing the different regimes in order to objectively weigh their advantages and disadvantages, contains even less specific information than *Humanisme et Terreur.* Out of 330 pages I do not think there are more than half a dozen that would allow a reader who was not a professional philosopher to clearly grasp the point of these subtle analyses or the purpose of this long discussion.

In *Les Aventures de la dialectique,* it is easy to distinguish three themes or rather three critiques: a critique of *dialectical materialism,* that is, of orthodox Communism; a critique of Sartre's *ultra-Bolshevism,* that is, of the justification of Communist practice which Sartre offers in terms of his own philosophy; and finally, spelled out at the end but underlying the book from beginning to end, a critique of the earlier positions of Merleau-Ponty himself.

These three critiques are not rigorously connected; at any rate, one does not follow from the other. I have no difficulty subscribing to the critique of Communist orthodoxy, a critique which resembles the one which Sartre himself made in *Matérialisme et Révolution;* or to the critique of Merleau-Ponty's *Humanisme et Terreur,* especially since it repeats arguments which I myself used seven years ago. But in its philosophical part, the chapter on Sartre's ultra-Bolshevism seems open to question.[1]

The political ideas in *Les Aventures* are not particularly original in themselves; they do not pretend to be. As Madame de Beauvoir would say, "They are in all of Aron's books." But perhaps it is not without importance that they should be expressed today by an intellectual whose loyalty to the left is unimpeachable and who rejects anti-Communism. In this sense this book, appearing ten years after the end of the war, may well mark the return of philosophers to common sense, the discovery that the French have a better chance to improve the lot

---

[1] The tone in which Mme. de Beauvoir replies to Merleau-Ponty is disagreeable and, in several instances, discourteous. But Sartre's tone in *Les Communistes et la paix* was not a well-mannered one either.

of mankind by trying to reform institutions than by dreaming of universal revolution.

From Marxist *Attentisme* to A-Communism

The political position of Merleau-Ponty seven years ago was one which he himself referred to as *"attentisme marxiste."* Today it is one of "a-Communism." Each of these positions is justified by an analysis of the present situation and a certain interpretation of history.

Seven years ago the central idea was the identification of Marxism with Historical Reason, which made it necessary to maintain a favorable prejudice toward the Soviet Union or to accord it a period of grace.[2]

On the political level, this "wait-and-see" policy did not result in allegiance to the Soviet camp, the American side, or even to the third party; in France and in the world, it tended to promote *nonwar* between Communists and anti-Communists. This attitude, Merleau-Ponty remarked in a statement to which too little attention has been paid, "assumed that the Soviet Union was not seeking to spread its regime to other countries by means of force. . . . If, tomorrow, the USSR threatened to invade Europe and established a government of its choice in all countries, another question would be raised and would have to be considered. Today this question does not arise."[3] The Korean war raised it, and since then the identification of Marxism with Historical Reason has been exposed or denounced as a survival of Kantism.

Let us first consider the new political stance. "The Soviet

2 The identification of Marxism with Historical Reason was based on the following line of argument: Humanity is achieved only when men recognize each other mutually; as long as there are masters and slaves, this recognition is impossible; only the proletariat, true intersubjectivity, is capable of going beyond these alternatives. It is not demonstrated that the Soviet Union, under the leadership of the Communist party, is creating a homogeneous society, that the proletariat is being transformed into a universal class and is achieving humanity; but since no other class can perform this task for the proletariat, it is well to keep giving the Soviet Union the benefit of the doubt, in other words, to be lenient toward the present Soviet reality in view of the future which the revolutionary plan is trying to create.

3 *Humanisme et Terreur*, p. 202.

Union put an end to the Korean war; she could no doubt have prevented it; and seeing that she did not prevent it and that it turned into military action, our attitude of sympathy became obsolete, because its meaning had changed. . . . Any advance of the USSR outside her frontiers would be supported by the struggle of the local proletariat, and if one decided to regard the matter each time as merely an episode in the class struggle, one would be lending her policy the very kind of backing she wanted."[4] To preserve the right to reject anti-Communism, it was necessary to criticize crypto-Communism or *progressisme*. "It was necessary, to be precise, that the rejection of the choice become the choice of a double rejection."[5]

I had not attached any importance to the statement that the question—that of the expansion of the Soviet Union outside her own frontiers—did not arise. Reasoning from the facts and from the official doctrine of the Soviet government, expressed in innumerable texts, I thought it obvious that the question did arise. The annexation of the Baltic States, the sovietization of the countries of eastern Europe—all these events were justified only by the Bolshevik philosophy, according to which the party which embodies the avant-garde of the world proletariat has the right to use the military force of the "Socialist bastion" to promote the seizure of power by the proletariats of other countries, in other words, by the Communist parties.

The Korean war represented a new phenomenon *on the diplomatic level,* in that for the first time a regular army, equipped with Soviet arms, crossed a line of demarcation drawn by agreement by the rulers of Washington and Moscow. All at once a local war broke out which gradually involved both North and South Korea, the United States, and China, and the risk, slim at first, but growing with Chinese intervention, of world war. Nevertheless, philosophically speaking, it does not seem to me that the event raised any problem that had not already been raised by the annexation of the Baltic States or the sovietization of eastern Europe. To be sure, the Red

4 *Les Aventures de la dialectique,* p. 308.
5 *Ibid.,* p. 310.

Army had entered Poland or East Germany to drive out the troops of the Third Reich and "liberate" the peoples from fascism. The *diplomatic* significance of this advance was in no way comparable to the crossing of the thirty-eighth parallel; but if you grant the Soviet Union the historical right to impose her own regime in Poland or Rumania, there is no reason to refuse her the same right in South Korea.[6]

Merleau-Ponty will object that at the time of Marxist *attentisme,* there were "neutral zones throughout the world, in Czechoslovakia, in Korea, where the two camps had come to terms with each other." I am afraid that these neutral zones did not exist objectively, but were created by an interpretation of the events which was itself dictated by a desire to avoid choice. Czechoslovakia would have been a neutral zone if the Communists there had agreed to a permanent division of power with the non-Communists, if Moscow had allowed diplomatic autonomy to Prague, but this was far from what happened. Stalin forbade the Czech government to accept participation in the Marshall Plan and the Communists seized total power when the date of the new elections was approaching. (They risked losing votes in comparison with the results of the elections held immediately following the liberation.) Perhaps Czechoslovakia would have avoided being taken over by the Soviet government if the non-Communists had been anti-Communists (i.e., if they had understood the objectives and methods of the Communists) .

In other words, Merleau-Ponty would have us believe that his wait-and-see policy toward the Soviet Union had "its objective conditions" immediately after the war, and that his present attitude is a response to changed conditions. I think, however, that he is mistaken, and that he is confusing his own uncertainties with a change in conditions. By a new irony of history, he is publishing this book and revealing his reaction to the "Korean period" of the cold war at a time when a post-

---

[6] The most "progressist" of the non-Communists do not question the fact that the Communists would have lost the free elections in Czechoslovakia, Rumania, and Poland: it was therefore military occupation by the Red Army that permitted sovietization.

Korean and post-Stalin period has already begun. For the first
time it is now possible to distinguish those neutral zones that
he dreamed of in 1948; the Soviet Union, for how long no
one can say, sincerely desires that *peaceful* coexistence which
the *attentistes* were bravely trying to promote at a time when
Stalin[7] was holding it up to ridicule.

Fortunately, Merleau-Ponty is, I think, unfair to his own
ideas, whose value does not depend on an interpretation of the
Korean war. The critique which he outlines of progressism
and crypto-Communism merely assumes that there is a power
struggle between the Communist and non-Communist coalitions, a fact which, in Europe at least, has been obvious to all
(except philosophers, perhaps) since 1945. Progressism consists in presenting what are, properly speaking, Communist
doctrines as if they were the spontaneous result of independent
reflection. It places a liberal trademark on a Marxist-Leninist
merchandise. But this practice in no way contributes to coexistence, which requires a balance of powers. How is Moscow to become cognizant of a resistance with which she must
reckon if, under the aegis of coexistence or of Marxist sympathies, the progressists are merely echoing Moscow propaganda
and subscribing to Soviet wishes?

Merleau-Ponty goes further and questions the exemplary
value of the Bolshevik type of revolution. Why should this kind
of revolution, which has succeeded only in pre-capitalist countries, be a model for post-capitalism? In a supreme heresy, he
does not shrink from the question, "Is the Czech proletariat
better off today than it was before the war?" which he answers
himself: "The fact that the question arises is sufficient evidence
that the great historical policy whose motto was the power of
the proletariat of all countries is itself called into doubt."[8] Let

---

[7] Stalin then wanted a *warlike* coexistence, not total war.

[8] *Les Aventures*, p. 301. "Because one has a certain idea about the true revolution, one decides that the USSR is not a revolution in that sense; one then
wonders whether the true revolution is not a dream; in the name of this doubt,
one retains the name of "revolutionary" for a regime which may arise; but since
this future is shrouded in uncertainty, one says merely that it will be a more
human social order." (p. 223) What Merleau-Ponty is criticizing in these lines
resembles his own attitude in 1948.

us add that the unanimity with which the progressist press admits that free elections in East Germany would give the majority to the supporters of Bonn also constitutes an answer of sorts.

It goes without saying that Merleau-Ponty tries to make a fundamental distinction between *a-Communism* and *anti-Communism*. Before analyzing this distinction and at the risk of blurring it hopelessly, I should like to recall the many and important points on which he has joined his critics of yesterday. He concedes that "to present Soviet Communism as the heir of Marxism"[9] is the best way to miss the truth of the Soviet Union; he concedes that one should compare Soviet and capitalist institutions as two real, imperfect, historical systems, and not transfigure Soviet institutions by relating them to the myth of the distant classless society; he concedes that "parliament is the only known institution which guarantees a minimum of opposition and of truth";[10] he concedes that the revolution was betrayed not through the fault of Stalin, or through the weakness of men, but by its own inner contradiction: "The peculiar property of a revolution is to believe itself absolute and not to be absolute precisely because of this belief."[11] We are delighted to hear these ideas, which would be typically "reactionary" from the pen of a reporter for *Le Figaro*, adopted by a man of the left.

Let us now consider the difference between *a-Communism* and *anti-Communism*. "A policy based on anti-Communism is ultimately a policy of war, and immediately a policy of regression; there are several ways of not being a Communist, and the problem has hardly been broached when one has said that one is not one."[12] The first part of this proposition is an unproved assumption (anti-Communism equals policy of war), the second part a common-sense truth which, curiously, contradicts the first.

[9] *Ibid.*, p. 301.
[10] *Ibid.*, p. 304.
[11] *Ibid.*, p. 298.
[12] *Ibid.*, p. 309.

If there are several ways of not being a Communist, why should anti-Communism be so defined, and likened to a policy of war? Let us consider the case of France. What is an anti-Communist? Simply a Frenchman who, believing that Parliament is the only institution that guarantees a minimum of opposition and truth and knowing that the Communist party, once in power, would abolish Parliament, opposes the seizure of power by the Communist party. In this sense Merleau-Ponty will grant that he is an anti-Communist. Perhaps he will reply that the question does not arise at the present time and that one should not take a position historically in relation to a question which is not of the present. The misadventures of Marxist *attentisme* should have taught Merleau-Ponty something about the dangers of choosing one's attitude only in relation to questions alleged to be of current relevance. But there is another, more direct answer. The question of the seizure of power by the Communist party does not arise precisely because there are, in France, a sufficient number of anti-Communists, that is, men who say *no* to the Communist plan. The philosopher can afford the luxury of neutrality, whereas others, ordinary citizens, forego the diploma of progressism in order to wage the battle of propaganda.

Things happen within nations very much the way they do on the international level: neutrality is possible on the condition that a balance is established between the coalitions. Yugoslavia and Austria owe their privilege of belonging to neither of the two blocs to the Western states, who have joined together to balance the Communist bloc. The a-Communists within the nation resemble the neutral parties of diplomacy. They sometimes perform a service, but they can be irritating when they affect a superiority over adversaries without whom they would not be free to express their detachment.

On the other hand, insofar as the adversaries inevitably incline toward a crude Manichaeism, the a-Communists have the merit of calling fanatics of both sides back to an awareness of themselves and a regard for the truth. It is well that intellectuals, whose commitment expresses itself by a rejection of all ties, should call to order those whom the heat of the battle might well lead to a single-minded clairvoyance or moralism. One does not define a policy by declaring oneself an anti-Communist. The concentration camps of Siberia do not excuse the slums of Billancourt. Nevertheless, the a-Communists would be wrong to suppose themselves equidistant from the two groups. They might conceivably occupy this median position if by anti-Communists one meant only McCarthyites for whom the hatred of the Red is a neurosis or a theme for demagogical exploitation. These extreme cases aside, the anti-Communist will never consider the a-Communist an enemy, as did the Communist of Stalin's day.

In December 1952, Nehru had, according to the strong language of Mr. Vishinsky, a choice between the role of agent of American imperialism and that of idealist or simpleton. Three years later, he is a hero of peace. A few years ago the Stalinist policy forbade or seemed to forbid the refusals to take sides, the intermediary positions, the various possibilities of abstention. Today, whether because this policy hopes to break down the Western alliance, or because it sees the noncommitted states as a force for peace, it treats neutral parties as friends, almost as allies. Indeed, the slogans of India or even of Yugoslavia are now beginning to resemble the Soviet slogans themselves—which does not imply, however, that they are contrary to Western interests.

Will it be the same within France? During Stalin's era doubt would hardly have been possible, and the non-Communist left of the Merleau-Ponty of 1955 would have been treated as an enemy, like the *Rassemblement démocratique révolutionnaire* of the Jean-Paul Sartre of 1948. Generally speaking, the Communists hate a non-Communist left much more than they hate anti-Communists. In the eyes of the Communists, the a-Communist is an anti-Communist. The Stalinist[13] wants to maintain the dogma that no improvement of the lot of the proletariat is

13 Even in the Bulganin-Khrushchev era.

possible within the context of capitalism. The fanatical anti-Communist should be grateful to the non-Communist left for its efforts to take the monopoly on progressism away from the Communist party and spread the slogans of reform among the working class.

A non-Communist left is not essentially related to the ideological attitude of a-Communism. In England the labor movement includes a non-Communist left similar to the one envisioned by Merleau-Ponty and *L'Express* as well as the virulent anti-Communism of the secretaries of labor unions. Attlee, Bevan, Morrison, and Gaitskell belong to the same party. If a large Socialist party existed in France, the author of *Les Aventures de la dialectique* might find himself in the same camp as the author of *L'Opium des intellectuels*.

The non-Communist left does not raise a universal problem; it raises a contingent problem, in France, because of the power of the Communist party and the weakness of the Socialist party. What are the elements of this problem in 1955, three years after the death of Stalin, now that the political temperature has become more moderate? According to precedent, in a phase like this one the Communist party should multiply its efforts to enter into the French community, to participate in the parliamentary game. It should, therefore, display some indulgence toward the non-Communist left, although continuing to denounce it mercilessly on the doctrinal level.

However this may be, the anti-Communist wishes the a-Communist luck in his search for a non-Communist left: the luck to garner enough votes to be neither absorbed by the Communist party if the latter proposes a common effort, nor paralyzed nor forced to the right if the Communist party declares war. In politics too, good luck sometimes means drawing to an inside straight.[14]

[14] One of the characteristics of a-Communism is supposedly the rejection of any means of force against Communism. In France nobody has proposed to outlaw the Communist party. But we refuse to establish as a principle that a party "which rejects the rule of the democratic game" *always* has a right to the same privileges as a party which respects this rule. The duty of suicide does not belong to the essence of parliamentary democracy.

The Failure of the Dialectic

The shift from Marxist *attentisme* to a-Communism, from the favorable prejudice toward the U.S.S.R. to the double rejection and the double critique, from unity of action or progressism to the non-Communist left, may be explained by a reflection upon the exigencies of coexistence and an analysis of the situation in France.

Merleau-Ponty does not confine himself to this historical self-scrutiny because he is a philosopher and also because he has changed philosophically, although nobody has noticed any connection between events—the Korean war—and his abandonment of the philosophical premises that underlay *Humanisme et Terreur*.

The 1948 book, to use the vocabulary of Merleau-Ponty himself, placed the whole of human history in the perspective of the proletarian revolution, a concept that included that of "universal class" or "true intersubjectivity" and that of a homogeneous society, that is, the mutual recognition of men or the disappearance of the opposition between masters and slaves. To judge the conformity of Soviet society to the revolutionary idea three criteria were utilized: socialist foundation (or collective ownership), internationalism, and spontaneity of the masses.

Now, in *Les Aventures de la dialectique,* all the concepts are thrown overboard, as it were. In 1948, if Marxism were not true, if the dialectic did not lead to the classless or homogeneous society, history would become a meaningless tumult. In 1955, the classless society and the very notion of the end of history or prehistory have been sacrificed without the author's giving way to despair. It is no longer a question of the privileges of the proletariat, "the only true intersubjectivity." After having provided the "intelligentsia" of the left with its philosophical security, he suddenly seems to be liberated from the superstitions he has done so much to foster.

The proletariat remains a class which is appeased and exploited and consequently disposed to revolt. But this revolt, if victorious, will re-establish a social structure, an economic regime, a political hierarchy. Will the post-revolutionary society be better or worse than the prerevolutionary society? The question is debatable, and perhaps no general proposition on this subject is valid. What matters philosophically is to compare *post*-revolutionary society with *pre*-revolutionary society rather than to compare pre-revolutionary society with the Revolution itself. But, one is tempted to wonder, how was it ever possible to compare an established society with the Revolution? How could such an error have been committed by so subtle a philosopher?

Philosophically speaking, this error seems to have had two sources: the unique dignity attributed to the proletariat, the universal class (or the class capable of becoming universal), and the unique dignity attributed to the Revolution, "permanent, critical of power," capable of transcending itself instead of crystalizing into institutions. Why did Merleau-Ponty attribute to the proletariat a peculiar virtue which he seems to refuse it today or which he seems to have forgotten? Why does he dream today of that "sublime point" which would resolve the contradictions, that point "from which matter and spirit would be indistinguishable, like subject and object, individual and history, past and future, discipline and judgment,"[15] even though he has ceased to believe that history could sustain it?

According to Marx, the proletariat is the last oppressed class which will surpass oppression at the same time as it surpasses itself. Why is it invested with this historic mission? In the youthful writings the reason invoked seems to be a philosophical one. The proletariat will destroy the class society because it embodies the dissolution of all classes; it will realize universal society because it embodies the obliteration of all particularities. In the later texts, after *The German Ideology* and *The Communist Manifesto*, the argument becomes more prosaic, apparently simpler. All previous revolutions have re-established a privileged class because they were made by a minority and therefore created a new oppressed class. The pro-

15 *Les Aventures*, p. 99.

letarian revolution, then, will not be the work of a minority, will not create a new oppressed class. In this sense, with the victory of the proletariat, oppression will overcome itself.

Not so long ago Merleau-Ponty assumed, rather than demonstrated, the universality of the proletariat. Today he no longer mentions it: ultimately proletarian intersubjectivity, however genuine, does not solve the problem of history. What becomes of proletarian intersubjectivity in a regime which claims to represent the proletariat? In order to demonstrate that there is no longer an oppressed or exploited class in a society of the Soviet type, one would have to make an analysis of the economy based on collective ownership, an analysis which Merleau-Ponty would probably consider external to the proper task of philosophy.

Existentialism, according to Merleau-Ponty, is a description of human existence. History is one of the dimensions of existence, and the two books are contributions to a phenomenology of the historical dimension of human existence. The basic assumptions of this description are, in part, the ones that Marx has chosen: man is in history at once subject and object, knowing and acting. He does not grasp the whole of history, his view of the past is determined by his desire for the future; he is never pure actor because he always endures the weight of things, never pure passivity because he always retains a fragment of his freedom.

Insofar as he defines knowledge of the past in terms of man as a part of history, Merleau-Ponty is returning to the perspectivism which he analyzed in *La Phénoménologie de la perception* and which had found favor with philosophers critical of history. This perspectivism of knowledge seems to lead to a relativism of values and goals. This relativism would be overcome if individual and collectivity came together, that is, if the society became true intersubjectivity, if action, instead of being limited by the particularity of a person or a period, were universalized by the universality of its objective. In other words, Merleau-Ponty is asking historical reality to be creative of truth, which by its nature eludes a creature who is located in and, in a sense, defined by history. History can be creative of truth only on the condition that it is human reality and not object, an exchange between "objective situation" and "human discussions," in other words, that it be at the point of junction "between subject, being, and other subjects."[16] If Merleau-Ponty has so much trouble defining the dialectic, it may be because as he understands it the dialectic is only a fiction or, if you prefer, the imagined solution to the contradictions which are inseparable from the human condition.

The distinction between a formal and a material sense of the dialectic will throw light on the question. Formally speaking, history is a dialectic characterized by the inclusion of the subject in the object, the creative response of man to a situation which is itself the crystallization of human works or acts. The essence of the dialectic is therefore "neither the idea of reciprocal action, nor that of a development which reactivates itself, nor the appearance of a quality which introduces into a new order a change which has heretofore been quantitative."[17] These, according to Merleau-Ponty, are consequences or aspects of the dialectic. Actually, all these traits characteristic of growth result from what essentially defines human action, which is a creative response to a situation which is itself the residue or consequence of a previous response and which nevertheless exists outside of each individual consciousness.

The dialectical (in the formal sense) nature of historical reality does not solve the problem raised by the perspectivism of all historical knowledge and the resulting particularity of all action. A philosophy that is critical in the Kantian sense tries to determine what our action should be by referring to abstract criteria or to a moral idea. A philosophy in the Hegelian tradition claims to find in the historical totality the solution to the contradiction between the uncertainty of every decision and the effort toward truth.

In the concept of the dialectic, Merleau-Ponty combines a description of man in history which is acceptable to all philoso-

16 *Ibid.*, p. 273.
17 *Ibid.*

phers of historicity (Dilthey as well as Hegel, Max Weber as well as Scheler) with a search for the final solution which would overcome the contradictions themselves. This search is related to Hegelian or Marxist thought, but is difficult to reconcile with existentialism.

In *Humanisme et Terreur* Merleau-Ponty postulated a "privileged state" which determines the meaning of the whole past because it is the necessary condition for the rationality of history. But this privileged state—homogeneous society or mutual recognition—was so formalized and generalized that it was impossible to relate it to a particular society. Merleau-Ponty decreed that only the proletariat was capable of achieving this "privileged state" by the seizure of power and the construction of a collective economy. But the weakness of the link between the historical particularities (proletariat, seizure of power, collective economy) and the "privileged state" resulted from the fact that formalized Marxism remained eternally true even if history did not realize it. But history, if it was capable of being wrong, was not by its nature creative of truth. We were no longer in the realm of Hegel, but of Kant.

In *Les Aventures de la dialectique* Merleau-Ponty approaches the same problem by another route. History will itself give proof of its truth at the moment when subject and object, decision and situation, past and future, individual and collectivity come together in the actual Revolution, when the proletariat recognizes the party as the expression of its will and its own action as critical and self-critical at the same time. "There is a resolution of the dilemma in practice because praxis is not subject to the postulate of theoretical consciousness, the rivalry of consciousnesses."[18]

Merleau-Ponty has no trouble discovering that this "resolution of the dilemma in practice," this "sublime point" in relation to which all history is placed in perspective, cannot last, and that the antinomies of theoretical consciousness and of the plurality of consciousness inevitably reappear.

It seems, according to our author, that these "perfect mo-

18 *Ibid.*, p. 69.

ments" really do exist.[19] "To be sure, there are moments, justly called revolution, when the inner mechanism of history causes the proletarians in their party and the workers and the peasants in the community to live the destiny which the dialectic assigns to them on paper, so that the government is none other than the representative of the people: we are then at that sublime point of which we have several times spoken. It is always in relation to these perfect moments that Trotsky places everything in perspective." "But this miraculous harmony is destroyed, the proletariat disperses, the party becomes or reverts to an instrument of control and coercion; it is only in principle, in a few privileged moments in history that criticism is incarnated in history and becomes a way of life. The rest of the time it is represented by functionaries."[20] After these perfect moments, ordinary life begins again—*Veralltäglichung der Revolution*, Max Weber would have said. Another society, another regime is born which could never sustain the revolutionary absolute, permanent criticism, negativity in action.

Moreover, even Marx was not able to confine himself to the reconciliation of contraries in praxis. During the second half of his life he seems to have forgotten that the dialectical praxis was not a simple action in the technical sense of the term, but a negativity, a negation of the given and a creation of truth, that the proletariat would put an end to classes and their struggles only if it was itself this point of junction of subject and object at which it overcame the antimonies by overcoming itself. But as soon as the dialectic is projected into things, as soon as some pseudo-nature fulfills the stages of history according to necessity, the dialectic vanishes or, at least, it is reduced to the half-mythological representation of an objective process which would spontaneously achieve resolution and reconciliation.

Thus Merleau-Ponty ends in a curious difficulty. Politically,

19 It is curious that Merleau-Ponty uses (*Ibid.*, p. 122) this expression which Sartre had used in an entirely different sense in *La Nausée*.

20 Sartre has stated the same idea in his *Critique de la raison dialectique*. The unified group, the pure act, are doomed to be crystallized in institutions, to relapse into the practico-inert.

at the end of the book, he gives notice, as it were, to the Revolution. "The question arises as to whether there is not more future in a regime which does not mean to remake history from the foundation, but only to change it, and whether it is not this regime that we must seek instead of entering once again into the circle of revolution."[21] Every revolution is betrayed because the decline of fervor is inevitable: a new elite is established, the party becomes a bureaucracy. There is no permanent revolution which would be criticism in power or the proletariat transcending itself. But from another point of view, those perfect moments in relation to which Trotsky placed the whole past in perspective are revolutionary explosions. Must we therefore sacrifice *politically* those moments which would resolve the contradictions *philosophically?*

It will be said that the illusion was "to seize upon a historical fact—the birth and growth of the proletariat—and invest it with the total significance of history. . . . It was to believe that the proletariat alone constituted the dialectic, and that the enterprise of putting it in power, temporarily removed from any dialectical judgment, could put the dialectic in power."[22] We have dispensed with the myth of a revolution which would itself embody the truth because it would be the power of interrogation and criticism. We have brought Communism back down to earth; we have, with considerable common sense, discovered that it is necessary to compare regimes among themselves. But then what remains of the dialectic? Precisely what we called the formal definition: the creative reaction of consciousness to the situation, the dialogue between conscious beings which forms the basis of historical reality. The attempt to find the truth of history in a permanent revolution or in the proletarian praxis has failed, just as the attempt to relate the past as a whole to some "privileged state" which would be homogeneous society, failed before it.

These failures are not without profit: they weed out myths and open the way for reasonable thought and action. But philo-

21 *Les Aventures*, p. 279.
22 *Ibid.*, p. 276.

sophically Merleau-Ponty has not so much gone beyond Marxism as retreated this side of it. History, according to him, is indeed a struggle of consciousness, the recovery and negation of what is inherited, but in its present stage philosophy provides us with neither a basis for values, nor a determination of the essentially human activities, nor a knowledge of the structure of the evolutionary process—nothing which would help us find our bearings in what can still be called the dialectic, but an open and scattered dialectic which does not look forward to any reconciliation either in a Kantian idea of Reason (homogeneous society) or in a proletarian praxis.

Have we not reached the extreme limit in the perspectivism of historical knowledge, the extreme limit in the particularism of action?

The Intolerable Dilemma

Why have we reached this point? Personally, I am inclined to believe that Merleau-Ponty is mistaken about the nature of his thought. He wants it to be historical and concrete, but he is wrong to deny the Kantian heritage on which it depends. The error of *Humanisme et Terreur* was not that it brought in the idea of recognition, but that it confused this idea with a forthcoming (or final) stage of the historical movement. The error consisted in linking indissolubly a particular term (the proletariat, the collective economy) with a universal, supra-historic term (the classless society). But if one rejects the universal (recognition) along with the particular (revolutionary proletariat, permanent revolution), what does man have left to guide his action?

The young Marx, whose writings are invoked by Merleau-Ponty, did not face this dilemma. Beginning with the Hegelian system, which he regarded as true, he had the advantage of a philosophical anthropology in terms of which history acquired unity through the years as it moved toward the final synthesis. He asked himself how consistent present history was with rational history. Probably Marx did not feel that he was adopting the Hegelian anthropology as such, but that he was modifying the relations of labor and war and placing in the center of the historical dialectic man, who manufactures his tools and creates his milieu by his labor. Man is alienated in present society, and the origin of this alienation is wage earning: the philosophical meaning of the proletarian revolution was therefore given from the start, and what primarily concerned Marx was the degree to which capitalist society, by its contradictions and its development, made inevitable the revolt of the proletariat against its enslavement, the revolt of man against his alienation.

Merleau-Ponty sees any projection of the dialectic into the social quasi-nature as a failure to recognize the true inspiration of Marxism. It seems to me that he is confusing two procedures, of which one is legitimate and the other is not. The dialectical conception of history is difficult to reconcile with the materialist metaphysic, and Sartre, after many others, has shown the ambiguities of materialism, which oscillates between realism (primacy of the object), a sketchy metaphysic (the brain produces thought), and an even sketchier epistemology (thought as reflection). If Marxism is an interpretation of the significant totality of history, it is not compatible with a philosophy which knows only matter, scattered into atoms. But the objectification of the dialectic is not in itself contradictory. Indeed, it is important that the massive social realities—forces of production, relations of production, the functioning of capitalism—create the conditions in which the proletariat will be incited to accomplish its revolutionary task. If the economic and social quasi-nature did not spontaneously tend toward the revolutionary situation, the proletarian negation would appear unforeseeable, arbitrary. For history to be comparable to a dialogue in which Reason has the last word, it is necessary that the questions be as reasonable as the answers, that the situations created by the past answers or the things themselves be as reasonable as the decisions.

No doubt Marx himself is at the limit of the contradiction: if the revolution and the proletarian victory are inevitable, what is the role of freedom? If there is an element of proletarian freedom, the outcome is not inevitable. It is not illegitimate, however, to find in Marxism a synthesis of quasi-necessity and freedom. The forces and relations of production evolve spontaneously toward a state in which the proletariat will realize its destiny only by Revolution—which allows for the possibility that the proletariat will betray itself while at the same time granting the proletarian revolt a kind of rationality.

Merleau-Ponty does not succeed in integrating into his interpretation of history either the analysis of social structures or the determination of the essential facts by reference to an anthropology. Everything proceeds as if these two dimensions, decisive as they are, were external to philosophical thought as he conceives it.

This accounts for his curious approach to the development of Marxist theory itself, the Marxism of Lukács being dubbed "Western Marxism" and the youth of Marxism. Western Marxism was in fact the Marxism of the Second International, the Marxism of which Kautsky was the moving spirit and the socialist parties, especially German social democracy, the agent of execution. In 1914 this Marxism was dealt a blow from which it has never recovered. It was defined by a belief in an objective dialectic which did not forbid the organized class, that is, the socialist party, to support the demands of the working class and to become established within the capitalist society. Marxism, at this period, sanctioned the belief that the Revolution was being prepared for an unforeseeable date, meanwhile engaging in a strictly reformist movement.

After 1914 the hesitation between reform and revolution took the form of the alternative between Communism and social democracy. Intellectuals with revolutionary tendencies could not espouse social democracy, whose bourgeois tendencies were obvious, but they found it difficult to subscribe to Bolshevik orthodoxy, since the materialism of Lenin and his companions was crude and, for a moderate philosopher, unacceptable. Lukács' *History and Class Consciousness* was, in Germany, the first and perhaps the only attempt to develop a philosophy that justified Communism without confining itself to the official formulas (thought as reflection, a rigorously objective dialectic built into the course of events, based on a materialistic philosophy, yet including the totality and providing the ultimate meaning of human history) . Lukács published his book even before all the youthful writings of Marx were known. But one need only refer to Hegel's *Phenomenology* to anticipate the dialectical (in Lukács' and Merleau-Ponty's sense) interpretation of Marx, in which the accent is placed on the role of the proletariat, which is at the same time subject and object, rather than on the contradictions between the forces and relations of production. As a matter of fact the Bolsheviks have never admired the theories of Lukács, who lived in the Soviet Union for a long time without publishing anything. Since the end of the Second World War he has been living in Hungary, where he is tolerated with indifference during liberal periods and forced to censor himself, compelled to self-criticism whenever the party has an attack of ideological severity. Faithful to Communism, about which he has very few illusions, he has, like a true philospher, given it a respectable façade. He has succeeded in developing one of those personal interpretations of Communism which make it possible to find a meaning in orthodoxy and to live a double life, externally a believer, inwardly a skeptic, but one who is not resigned to losing his faith.

This Hegelianized Marxism derived from the youthful writings of Marx does not necessarily lead to a lukewarm Bolshevism. Others, beginning with the same texts, have been inclined toward social democracy. Still others, like Merleau-Ponty, have remained outside of the two parties, wavering between Marxist sympathy (alliance with Communism) and the non-Communist left. For the past ten years Merleau-Ponty and the existentialists have relived the spiritual crisis of European philosophers or scholars who are temperamentally attracted to Marxism but repelled by the crudeness of the Leninist or Stalinist dogma. Far from being representative of "Western Marxism," Lukács is the creator of ideological subtleties which help Western intellectuals to rejoin Soviet Marxism.

Since the events of 1914 and 1917, the division of the Second International into national parties, and the seizure of power by the Communist party, there have been, historically, only two paths between which it has been necessary to choose: the path of revolution, in liaison with the Soviet Union, and the path of social democratic reform, within the national framework. In most Western countries the majority of intellectuals and workers have chosen the second path. Between the two world wars Germany, after the Second World War Italy and France, went through the crisis of the necessary and impossible choice. Subordination to the Soviet Union is a caricature of true internationalism; but how much internationalism is there in social democratic reformism? Class consciousness is almost as absent from the Bolshevik cult of the party as it is from the banality of the labor unions or of the parties dedicated to the immediate improvement of the lot of their faithful followers.

Politically, a return to the young Marx is of no help. One rediscovers the philosophical themes which, before 1848, and especially before 1845, inclined the mind of Marx toward the proletariat, a totally deprived class which cannot overcome itself without at the same time overcoming all exploitation. During the remainder of his life, Marx appeared to lose interest in the philosophical foundations and ethical reasons underlying his revolutionary desire, and tried to trace in reality the path that would be followed by reason. If the dialectic—contradictions and final synthesis—was not an integral part of the social quasi-nature, then the historic mission of the proletariat as a universal class, or the unique character of the proletarian revolution, became ideologies. It was historical reality itself that was to decide whether the anthropological dialectic conceived by Marx was the dream of a young man or the inspiration of a prophet. One century after writing, the *Economic and Philosophic Manuscripts* sheds no light on the present situation. The elements that were combined in Marx's scheme of history have now become separated, and the philosophical texts can justify a reluctant acceptance of Bolshevism as well as a resigned acceptance of social democracy.

Merleau-Ponty, too, has just completed the itinerary which starts with the revolutionary situation and goes back to the youthful writings of Marx, only to return to the present. But he has not found the answer to the questions that plagued him. Politically, he has come round to a non-Communist left which would play the parliamentary game—one modality among others, of the choice of social democracy. This modality, like any others, is open to debate, but the debate should be political and historical: what is the meaning of this left at a given date, in a given country? Philosophically, he has arrived at the end of his odyssey convinced that Marx himself was the first to betray the dialectic. It was Marx who, as far back as 1848, projected the dialectic into the object and created the monster of "dialectical materialism."

There is no doubt that one can find numerous passages by Marx and Engels which justify this criticism. In his maturity or old age, Marx seems indeed to have believed that the class struggle was a variety of the struggle for survival characteristic of the biological order. He has expressed himself as if the economic contradictions unfolded their consequences in the manner of a natural determinism. The dialectic, interpreted in materialist terms, does indeed cease to be what Merleau-Ponty wants it to be—the meaningful unfolding of events thanks to human action, which overcomes the contradictions between object and subject, individual and collectivity, past and future. It breaks down into fragmentary decisions and particular actions unless one succeeds in grasping the structure of the real and the major activities of the historical subject. The historical process should present the articulateness provided by the objectification of the dialectic (structured unity of each regime or period, contradictions within the structure of which the class struggle is the expression, contradictions resolved in the following regime, etc.). Without this structure, which is an expression of human nature or social nature, one runs the risk of ending in the pure and simple intersubjectivity that had been described by phenomenology at the outset.

Such, it seems to me, is Merleau-Ponty's position. In renouncing revolutionary ecstasy, he also renounces those sublime points when action reconciles the contraries. History, according to the interpretation of Max Weber, offers him partial wholes, partial totalities. But Max Weber knew that his philosophy was a critique, that his decision went beyond all rationality. Merleau-Ponty, not having discovered, in the course of his adventures, either the principles of an anthropology or the structure of the historical process, having thrown overboard the formalism of mutual recognition and the classless society, having lost faith in the "perfect moments" of revolutionary action, finally asks the economist to develop a general economics and to help him choose his path.

L'Etre et le néant

The polemic of the Merleau-Ponty of 1955 against the Merleau-Ponty of 1948, the shift from Marxist *attentisme* to a-Communism, would probably not have aroused so much comment if *Les Aventures de la dialectique* did not include a hundred-page chapter on Sartre and ultra-Bolshevism. Merleau-Ponty vs. Sartre: to its delight, the philosophical left found itself torn between its two masters. An unhealthy curiosity about the private lives of writers added to the interest of a dialogue between the two champions of existentialism.[23]

Merleau-Ponty's polemic has a strange quality. For several years Sartre, without belonging to the Communist party, has been associated with its activities. Merleau-Ponty has followed another path, whence his criticism of the Sartrian position of active alliance without party membership. This properly political discussion does not occupy much space in the chapter. Most of it is devoted to a double demonstration. Sartre has a precise theory of present-day Bolshevism or ultra-Bolshevism, but the agreement between Sartre's philosophy and Communist practice carries a condemnation of both practice and philosophy, for each has sacrificed the supreme wealth of the dialectic.

23 That in our generation no friendship has withstood differences of political opinion, that friends have had to change their political allegiance together in order to remain friends, is both understandable and unfortunate.

I said that this demonstration is strange. The political position of Sartre is recent: the philosophical ideas which, according to Merleau-Ponty, serve him as a foundation, have a long
history. One has trouble believing that the ontology of *L'Etre
et le néant* necessarily leads to the articles on *Les Communistes
et la paix.* No doubt this is not exactly Merleau-Ponty's thesis,
since he insists upon the originality of each of Sartre's works in
relation to the ones that preceded it. Nevertheless, there is said
to be a pre-established harmony between the Sartrian ontology
of pure will, of insular consciousness, and the Bolshevik practice of the act which, by a mysterious and unjustifiable fiat,
brings forth the party from the scattered mass. This ontology
did not necessarily lead Sartre to an alliance with Communism,
but once allied with the Communists, it gave him a way of integrating Communism with his own goal, of interpreting the
Communist action within the framework of a philosophy which
assumes the irreducible opposition of the subject and the
Other, the formless class and the unified party, things and men,
but ignores the dialectic by which the apparently opposed
terms come together.

Let us return to our distinction between *formal dialectic* and
material dialectic, or, in other words, between the dialectical
(or dialogue-like) character of relations between consciousnesses and the possible totalization of this evolution of consciousnesses at odds with one another and with humanized
things. Is the human world as seen by Sartre formally dialectical in the sense that Merleau-Ponty attributes to this word?
The answer seems, by all evidence, affirmative.

It is excessive to maintain that Sartre ignores "that interworld between men and things which we call history, sym-
bolism, truth in the making."[24] It is easy to quote, as Mme.
de Beauvoir does, many passages in which Sartre explicitly
recognizes this interworld—objective, presenting itself to man
almost as an *en-sei*, although charged with human significances.
For example: "We dominate matter by means of work, but the

[24] *Les Aventures,* p. 269.

milieu dominates us in turn by the crystallized profusion of the thoughts which we have inscribed upon it."[25]

Similarly, it is true that all meanings are dictated by consciousness, that "the act of consciousness is an absolute and gives the meaning."[26] Sartre everywhere recognizes the ambiguous meanings which are inseparable from the facts, which consciousness neither creates nor constructs, which the subjects discover and in which they exist.

Similarly too, Sartre recognizes another relation between the I and the Other besides that of the gaze which leaves individuals face to face without communication. He has no intention of denying "the existence of those mediatory regions among the various subjects which are known as culture, literature,"[27] and which Hegel called "objective mind." To be sure the social never determines consciousness in the same way the milieu determines the work in the conception of Taine. As a matter of fact, Sartre and Merleau-Ponty interpret the relation between situation and writer (or philosopher or political man) in exactly the same way. "The social field appears at the same time before and behind it (consciousness) and it could not be otherwise, since in Sartre past and future are inseparably intertwined."[28]

If objective meanings exist, if there is not only a plurality of subjects but intersubjectivity, if there is an interworld, it is difficult to see why Sartre should deny history. He has never failed to recognize that the historian is himself a part of history or that there is an evolution of meaning in institutions, or that historical wholes are real and that the self is formed within the limits set by the combination of circumstances into which we are born:

The historical whole at every moment determines our powers, it fixes limits to our field of action and to our real future, it conditions our attitude toward the possible and the impossible, the real

25 Quoted by Mme. de Beauvoir in the June–July 1955 issue of *Les Temps modernes,* p. 2078.
26 *Les Aventures,* p. 156.
27 Quoted by Mme. de Beauvoir, *op. cit.,* p. 2082.
28 *Ibid.,* p. 2083.

and the imaginary, what is and what should be, time and space; after this, we in turn determine our relations with others, that is, the meaning of our life and the value of our death; it is within these limits that our *Me* finally appears. It is history which shows some people a way out and causes others to mark time in front of closed doors.[29]

If this is the case—if history, as interpreted by Sartre, involves precisely, as in the interpretation of Merleau-Ponty, the objective meaning of things, the evolution of meanings in institutions, intersubjectivity, the intermediary regions of culture, the reality of sociality—then why has Merleau-Ponty, whose good faith is not open to doubt, misunderstood this aspect of Sartre's thought?

Mme. de Beauvoir, at the end of her article, gives a first reason. Some of the statements that Merleau-Ponty attributes to Sartre, applying them to the *Me* or the *person* or the historical subject, would be true if they were taken, on the level of ontology, as referring to the *pour-soi* or to consciousness, the pure presence in itself. It is true that the *pour-soi* is originally the principle of all revelation and that the world, in this sense, is coextensive with it. It is true that consciousness—*Erlebnis*—is all translucidity and discovers the Other only under the gaze which objectifies itself. In certain respects the *ontological* description of consciousness is opposed to the *ontic* description of men engaged in history. It is as if Merleau-Ponty thought he had found, in the ontological description of *L'Etre et le néant* an explanation for certain historical and political attitudes which puzzled him. But instead of giving these references to ontology as a possible explanation—more psychological than philosophical—for the theory of the party and of action, he has reconstructed a Sartrian *ontics* of the human condition based on these fragments of ontology—an ontics which Sartre has every right to reject.

In Sartre's *Les Communistes et la paix*, class does not exist outside the party; the proletariat cannot turn its back on the party, because the proletariat exists as a class only as unified

29 *Ibid.*, p. 2089.

in and by the party. Only another party besides the Communist party could release the proletariat from its position of dependence. Ultimately, it seems that the party is a pure act which, in the manner of freedom, sweeps down on the formless mass and transforms passivity or dispersion into creative will. Moreover, the Communist action seems revolutionary without any visible connection with an overall movement of history, a negation of the given and of present society without being a sure affirmation of the classless society. The relation of class to party, of revolutionary action to historical truth: these are the two areas in which Merleau-Ponty perceives an affinity between Bolshevik practice and Sartrian ontology.

On the first point—*class and party*—certain passages in *Les Communistes et la paix* are close to what Mme. de Beauvoir calls pseudo-Sartre. Sartre forbids the proletariat to reject the party unless it is united in another party—which reduces the existence of the class not organized into a party to a minimum. But, fundamentally, he wants class unity to be "neither passively received nor spontaneously produced."[30] Stated differently, he wants the relation of the workers to the party and of the masses to the leaders, to be dialectical: the leaders are nothing unless the masses follow them, the masses do not constitute a unity unless there is a party to consolidate them.

This brings us to the last point and certainly the most important: is history creative of truth? If the truth of history disappears, then the formation of the proletariat into a class by means of the party, however justified by events, is an arbitrary decision and history itself becomes "insofar as it is knowable, the immediate result of our wills, and for the rest, an impenetrable opacity."[31]

In what sense does Merleau-Ponty himself provide an answer to the question which he asks his friend—in other words, in what sense is history, as he interprets it, creative of truth? How does the event become its own criterion? As we have seen, Merleau-Ponty's answer fluctuates between reference to a formal idea—mutual recognition—and reference to those "perfect mo-

30 *Ibid.*, p. 2097.
31 *Les Aventures*, p. 134.

ments" when the doubts disappear because the antinomies are overcome. The Merleau-Ponty of 1955 has abandoned the formal idea as tainted with Kantism. He admits that the perfect moments are ultimately delusive, since once the "revolutionary ecstasy" is over, the self ceases to be identified with the Other, the class with the party, revelation with action, power with criticism. Consequently, although he retains the dialectic in the formal sense of the term, he has lost, as he explicitly admits, not only all notion of the end of the dialectic—the resolution of contradictions—but any way of avoiding the perspectivism of revelation and the particularity of action.

Has Sartre, too, renounced the fulfillment of man in and by Revolution? In this respect there has always existed a major difference between the two thinkers. The Marxism of Sartre was "ontic," not "ontological." It was difficult to understand how the quest for the classless society (on the ontic level) tallied with the ontological thesis of man as a "useless passion." Sartre knows *one* meaning which everyone freely gives to his life and his death; he does not know *the* meaning of *total history*, still less a meaning identified with a privileged state which would mark the end of history or of prehistory. But as Sartre is not unaware, the end of history or prehistory in Marxism signifies much more than an end desired by one person, several persons, or even a class; it marks a break in the course of human events, the shift from one type of society to another. Does Sartre place the past and its action in perspective by reference to this awe-inspiring and unprecedented event?

Yesterday as today, Sartre has always been more of a conqueror than a Roman. He has never doubted that his place was among the exploited who revolt against their condition, he has never shown any certainty about the conformity of the future society to the idea of a classless society. In this sense he believes in revolutionary negativity rather than in the affirmations implied by the negating action.

Does this mean that Sartre, as Merleau-Ponty charges, chooses revolution without knowing what he is choosing, with no justification other than the fact of present oppression?

It is true that the three installments of *Les Communistes*

et la paix are strangely vague on the points which should be clarified if sympathy to Communism (even without party membership) is to become philosophically and politically intelligible. To what degree is the Soviet regime faithful to the revolutionary idea? To what degree are the activities of the French Communist party oriented toward Revolution in the Marxist sense of word?

As long as the French Communist party wants to be the Soviet Union, it cannot serve both Revolution and coexistence. Peaceful coexistence between non-Communist and Communist countries is like peace between Catholics and Protestants: each group abandons the attempt to convert the other by force.

Nor does Sartre ask himself the question: Is the Soviet regime which is imposed from above on Poland and Rumania and which would be imposed on France if she were ever governed by the Communist party, is this regime the fulfillment of the revolutionary ideal?

That Sartre's choice of revolution seems politically ambiguous, without firm foundation, I am willing to accept. But the interpretation based on the ontology of freedom that Merleau-Ponty gives of it, does not convince me. Is the organized will of the party more important than the spontaneous will of the masses? Is the will of the party defined by a negation of the real without concrete determination of the post-revolutionary society? Certainly, but one finds these two elements in all Bolshevik theorists from Lenin to Sartre, for the simple reason that these theorists have always had their doubts about the revolutionary spontaneity of the masses.

On one point only one is tempted to agree with Merleau-Ponty and to explain Sartre's political opinion in terms of the ontology of *L'Etre et le néant*. Sartre has emphasized more than once that the meaning of a historical event depends on the intention of the actor. In order to show that the policies of the U.S.S.R. and the French Communist party are not revolutionary it would be necessary, according to Sartre, "to demonstrate that Soviet leaders no longer believe in the Russian revolution or that they think the experiment has resulted in failure." When one reads a statement of this kind one wonders why the intentions of the Soviet leaders should be the final criterion in determining the meaning of reality. I find it hard to believe that Sartre is unaware of the elementary distinction between objective meaning and subjective meaning, or regards the latter as unconditionally valid.

Because he insists on the uncertainty of historical judgments, Sartre is inclined to look for certainty in subjectivity (or intention). Since one can say anything at all about the Soviet Union, since the proletarian party is in power but at the same time concentration camps exist, where is one to find an incontestable meaning? If the revolutionaries no longer believed in the Revolution, the chips would be down, and what was in Russia would simply be one regime among others.

The same phenomenon, in reverse, appears in the judgments that Sartre passes on his adversaries. If an anti-Communist were to call Sartre a bastard for *desiring* the concentration camps, Sartre would protest—and legitimately—that he *desires* the Revolution, the liberation of the proletariat, and that the camps are the object neither of his desire nor of the Communist desire with which he declares himself to be in partial agreement. But he does not hesitate to accuse the anti-Communists of desiring colonial repression and police brutality. To resort to intention or purpose in order to interpret the actions of either extreme is undeniably very un-Communist, not very Marxist (unless this intention be the will of the class), and in itself unjustifiable. Our acts are part of the fabric of events and acquire meaning only in the consciousness of the other, although it is not true that the perception of the other determines their final meaning. From the outset the perception of the other is as valid as the intention of the actor, and in proportion as the comprehension of the observer broadens, embracing a more extended period of time, this comprehension becomes relatively more important than the initial purpose of the actor. Such ideas are so much the common property of Sartre and Merleau-Ponty (and of many others) that one cannot conceive of Sartre's forgetting them and according a privileged status to the decision of the conscience.

It may be said that at this level of politics we again encounter the Sartrian vacillation between *ontology* and *ontics*. The *pour-soi* is radically free, the person at every moment involved in the world. Perhaps Sartre sometimes yields to the temptation to resolve the ambiguity of historical meaning by going back to the absolute of consciousness; but this would be to commit an error against his own philosophy.[32] Personally, I would be inclined to explain the reference to intention in order to save some and damn others by the passion of Sartre the man rather than by the thought of Sartre the philosopher. The spontaneous moralism and unconscious Kantism of Sartre suddenly burst forth in statements which do not agree with his present sympathies.

If this analysis is accurate, Merleau-Ponty has given the advantage to Sartre's defenders in discussing *Les Communistes et la paix* in terms of the ontology of *L'Etre et le néant*. Sartre's political theory seems to me vulnerable for simple reasons which are very inferior to the one invoked by his adversary.

Sartre fluctuates between a sympathy, without membership, for the Communist party *hic et nunc* and a sympathy for the technique of action of the Communist party in general. Explicitly, he declares that he confines himself to a present decision, but in fact the arguments by which he tries to demonstrate the necessity of the party to promote the class to praxis and consciousness are in no way related to the situation in France. If they are valid, they are valid everywhere. But how is one to apply them to countries featuring advanced capitalism, where the workers and their elected leaders obstinately reject both action of the Bolshevik type and the doctrine of the seizure of power by a monolithic party? Sartre's mistake is not, as Merleau-Ponty would have it, that he places a Sartrian interpretation on the Communist action; Sartre's justification of the party, apart from terminology, does not differ so much from Lenin's. Sartre's mistake is to adopt the Leninist justification of 1903 without concerning himself with what has hap-

---

[32] On this point I was wrong. He continues to make this error in *La Critique de la raison dialectique*.

pened since then, i.e., the construction of Soviet society under the direction of the Communist party and the rejection of Bolshevik methods and, even more widely, of revolutionary methods by most of the proletariats of the Western world.

Europe being what it is, what can a Communist party do in the part of the old continent west of the Iron Curtain? Is it useful as opposition? Do we want to strengthen it so that it can more effectively paralyze the French government? Or do we hope that it will seize the power? And what consequences would a Communist victory in France have for the coexistence of the two worlds? These questions—not metaphysical but concrete, current—are ones that must be answered if we want to make a reasonable decision in 1955.

As long as Merleau-Ponty confines himself to simple and so to speak nonphilosophical objections, he is on solid ground. How is one to justify sympathy to the Communist party before one has explained the nature and meaning of the Soviet regime?[33] How is one to work at coexistence if, instead of criticizing both sides, one systematically gives one's approval to one? How long is the Communist party going to accept cooperation without membership? When Sartre, carried away by his torrential logic, gives his approval to the party that refuses opposition, is he not putting himself in the wrong? "Anyone who associates himself with the party without belonging to it cooperates in the action without subscribing to the idea."[34]

On the other hand, as soon as Merleau-Ponty criticizes Sartre's attitude philosophically he ceases to convince, because the unbiased reader has the impression that the author is just as vulnerable to attack as his opponent. He writes, for example, "Perhaps it does not make much sense to deal with Communism, which is an action, on the level of pure thought."[35] But every political philosopher thinks about the action of others, and thus deals with action by means of thought, and

[33] Mme. de Beauvoir, in her reply to Merleau-Ponty, exclaims virtuously, "What does the Soviet Union have to do with it?" Impossible to miss the unconscious humor.

[34] *Les Aventures*, p. 232.

[35] *Ibid.*, p. 237.

this thought, even if it does not result in a commitment, is in itself action. By interpreting an action one changes its meaning in the eyes of others, and in so doing one changes human reality: that is to say, one acts.

"The weakness of Sartre's position," writes Merleau-Ponty, "is that it is a position for someone living in the capitalist world, not for someone living under Communism which is, however, what it is about." But the a-Communism of Merleau-Ponty is open to the same reproach: if he lived on the other side of the Iron Curtain, he would not have the freedom to put the two blocs on the same level. But why should not either make use of the right accorded him by capitalist society?

Merleau-Ponty writes half of his book as if he were still a Marxist, the other half as if he no longer were: "Lenin never sacrificed spontaneity to consciousness; he postulated their agreement in the communal work of the party because he was a Marxist, that is, because he believed in a policy which proves its truth by becoming that of the proletarians."[36] But in this sense is Merleau-Ponty himself still a Marxist? "History is not the unfolding of a ready-made truth, but from time to time it has a rendezvous with a truth which is made, and which is recognized by the fact that the revolutionary class, at least, functions as a whole and that in this class social relations are not opaque like those of the classless society." These rendezvous with a truth which is made, this recognition of the truth by the proletarians, are the perfect moments when the antinomies are resolved. But Merleau-Ponty has given us two reasons to distrust these "perfect moments": they do not last, and the will of the proletariat is never inscribed in unambiguous characters upon flesh-and-blood proletarians. Even when they do recognize themselves in the action which the party suggests to them, they have been urged, influenced, sometimes compelled by the *other*—intellectuals, professional revolutionaries, the organization itself. The philosopher never loses the freedom to appeal to the empirical proletariat to be faithful to its vocation.

Having refused to set up the coincidence between proletariat

36 *Ibid.*, p. 173.

and party as a criterion of the truth, what right does Merleau-Ponty have to condemn Sartre for doing the same? Once this coincidence has been abandoned or held to be precarious, one possible path is that of Bolshevism—to subscribe to the authority of the party—the other, that of democracy—to place faith neither in the class nor in the party but invoke one or the other according to the circumstances. And it is still necessary, if one takes this second path, to retain the historical schema of Marx (contradictions of capitalism leading to the Revolution). We do not know about Sartre, but does Merleau-Ponty retain it any more than he?

I do not hold this against Merleau-Ponty, but I do criticize him for using against Sartre a philosophy that he has abandoned himself and for ignoring the current results of his research: the discovery that the dialectic of revelation and action involves a moment of objective knowledge. The perspectivism of historical interpretation, the ambiguities of comprehension lead to arbitrariness unless they are limited and controlled by a grasp of reality based on positive methods. Merleau-Ponty is becoming aware of this humble necessity for empirical investigation between spontaneous revolt and conscious action. He is beginning to see "a generalized economy of which Communism and capitalism would be particular cases."[37]

Scientific investigation would not offer us any conclusion as sweeping as that of Marxist pseudo-science. It would reveal neither the secret of total history nor the necessary coincidence of the desirable and the inevitable. It would permit that comparison of economic regimes whose function Merleau-Ponty perceives in a reasonable deliberation.

Simone de Beauvoir, on the other hand, does not let herself be betrayed into these subtleties of bourgeois "pluralist" thought. ("There is only one truth," she says with tranquil certainty.) Western society is entirely corrupted by the exploitation it inflicts on the working class; and when it does achieve certain values, it is all the more guilty. Synthetic

---

[37] He means a general theory of economics which would interpret the two regimes as species of a genus or variations on a theme.

thought—that of Marx, that of Sartre—discovers the essence of the capitalist order in exploitation. Péguy, too, said that a single injustice was enough to corrupt an entire society. At least he did not claim to speak as a "scientific socialist."

This kind of synthetic thought gives us pause. We are willing to attribute to God the capacity and to the primitive the habit of apprehending society as a whole, of making a judgment of it without preliminary analysis. One wonders what is the proper classification for minds capable of grasping the social whole without analyzing its elements.

Fanaticism, Prudence, and Faith

When one reviews the political attitudes of Sartre and Merleau-Ponty since 1945 one has the impression of having witnessed a kind of ballet or square dance. The "new left" of the Merleau-Ponty of 1955 resembles the *Rassemblement démocratique révolutionnaire* of the Jean-Paul Sartre of 1948. The Marxist *attentisme* of Merleau-Ponty was closer to the pre-pro-Communism of Sartre than to the a-Communism expounded in *Les Aventures de la dialectique*.

Since they are the professional philosophers, each justifies his current opinions by arguments which, if they were valid, would hold true for centuries. They are all the more inclined to elevate the episodes of their existence to the level of eternity because they are obsessed by the examples of Marx and Lenin. But existentialism, whether that of Sartre or that of Merleau-Ponty, is not an essentially historical philosophy.

From Existentialism to Doctrinarism

Sartre and Merleau-Ponty, in their pre-political work, belong to the tradition of Kierkegaard and Nietzsche and the revolt against Hegelianism. The individual and his destiny constitute the central theme of their reflection. They disregard that totality whose recognition by the philosopher marks the beginning of wisdom. Unfinished history imposes no truth. Man's freedom is the capacity of self-creation, although one cannot make out, at least in *L'Etre et le néant,* what law this creation should obey or toward what objective it should tend.

Every man must find the answer to the situation without deducing it from books or receiving it from others, and yet this answer imposes itself on the solitary and responsible actor. Authenticity—in other words, the courage to take responsibility for oneself, one's heritage, and one's talents—and reciprocity—the recognition of the other, the desire to respect him and to help him fulfill himself—these seem to be the two cardinal virtues of *homo existentialis*.

The existentialists describe human existence as it is lived, without this description referring to a historical particularity. To be sure, this description arises from experience and is related to the latter as the work is related to the artist, but its validity is not limited to one time. Whether it is a question of freedom or of authenticity, it remains true for all men throughout the ages that consciousness is fulfilled by liberating itself and is liberated by becoming responsible for itself.

De Waehlens dismisses as a "bad joke" the objection of Löwith, who quotes a student's remark, "I am resolved to do something, only I don't know what." He writes, "Philosophy, existential or otherwise, would destroy itself if, instead of teaching us to think, it pretended to provide everyone with formulas which, on every occasion, could resolve the problems of his life. The *Sein-Zum-Tode*, whatever else we may think of it, can only be an inspiration, a light by which everyone confronted by his situation has the duty and the privilege of deciding freely, without ceasing to run the risk of being wrong or even of being unfaithful."[1] The objection strikes me as little more than a bad joke. No philosophy can ever provide "formulas" for solving the problems raised by circumstances. But a philosophy which refers to an ideal of virtue or wisdom, to the categorical imperative or to good will, offers "an inspiration, a light" which are different from those offered by a philosophy which places the accent on freedom, choice, invention. If the philosopher does not know the meaning of virtue and enjoins his disciples to be themselves, is it so wrong of them to conclude that the act of resolution is more important than its content?

[1] *Une philosophie de l'ambiguité*, p. 306, note.

Having ruled out a moral law which would govern intention, resolved to ignore those virtues or that inner improvement which the Greeks or the Christians proposed as an ideal, the existentialists propose that each individual win his salvation according to his own law, and they avoid anarchy only by the idea of a comunity in which individuals would recognize each other reciprocally in their humanity.

The idea of the authentic community in a philosophy which puts the accent on the individual's creation of values and even of his own destiny seems to be an appeal to harmony against the reality of the clash of individuals, a dream of universality in a phenomenology of particular fatalities. In any case, this altogether formal idea is an idea of Reason (to use the Kantian vocabulary) ; it is not and cannot be the object of a singular will or the imminent end of the historical movement.

On the basis of this philosophy, should philosophers be favorable to a democracy in the Western style or a democracy in the Soviet style? In any case, they should not attribute an absolute value to either. Neither one wholly achieves the reciprocal recognition of individuals. As for which of the two comes closest to this ideal or deviates from it the least, this is a political or historical question which neither *L'Etre et le néant* nor *La Phénoménologie de perception* helps to answer. When it is a question of the status of ownership, the functioning of the economy, or the single or the multiple party system, sociological description is more instructive than transcendental phenomenology.

The Marxism of the two philosophers is partly accidental in origin. Both men, living west of the Iron Curtain, have found themselves hostile to bourgeois democracy and incapable of espousing orthodox Communism. But this political preference would not have found expression in philosophical writings if the temptation of Marxism had not influenced the heirs of Kierkegaard, if the existentialists, having begun with transcendental consciousness, fear and trembling, had not felt the need to reintegrate into a nonsystematic philosophy the fragments of the Hegelian-Marxist historical totality.

In Leo Strauss's *Natural Law and History*, at the end of the chapter on Burke, the author writes:

Political theory became the study of what practice has produced, the investigation of the real, and ceased to be the search for what should be; practical theory ceased to be "theoretically practical" (that is, deliberation at the second remove) and became purely theoretical in the sense in which metaphysics (and physics) had been traditionally understood as purely theoretical. It was then that there appeared a new type of theory or metaphysics whose highest theme was human activity and what it produces rather than the totality, which is in no sense the object of human activity. Within the totality and the metaphysic which is based on it, human activity occupies a distinguished but secondary place. When metaphysics began to regard human actions and their results as the end toward which all beings and all processes tend, metaphysics became the philosophy of history. The philosophy of history was essentially theory, that is, a contemplation of the practice of men and necessarily, therefore, of total and complete human practice; it presupposed that privileged human action, History, was complete. In becoming the highest theme of philosophy, practice ceased to be practice in the true sense, that is, the concern for *agenda*. The anti-Hegelian rebellions of Kierkegaard and Nietzsche, insofar as they exert a strong influence upon opinion today, thus appear as attempts to re-establish the possibility of a practice, that is, a human life which has before it a significant and indeterminate future. But these attempts increased the confusion, since they did all they could to destroy the very possibility of theory. "Doctrinarism" and "existentialism" appear to be two extremes equally tainted with error.

Sartre and Merleau-Ponty combine in a curious way the two attitudes which Leo Strauss calls the "extremes." In the manner of the doctrinaires, Merleau-Ponty (in 1948) and Jean-Paul Sartre (today) lean toward the unique truth of the classless society. They glorify revolution in the manner of the theoreticians denounced by Burke because they seem to ignore the historical diversities, the slow creations, the unforeseeable accidents, the innumerable variations on the same themes. But at the same time they belong among the descendants of Kierke-

gaard rather than those of Hegel since they regard individual
consciousness as the primary reality, the origin of all philosophy,
and since the historical totality—the total and complete human
practice—seems incompatible with their mode of thought. In
certain respects Marx and Nietzsche are "opposite extremes":
but by many paths their descendants come together.

Marx had reinstated the concern for *agenda,* that is, a "significant future," without renouncing the advantages provided
by "a total and complete human practice." All he had to do was
assert both that the future is unforeseeable, since the negating
action is the essence of humanity, and that the proletarian
revolution will make a fundamental break in the course of
human events. Nobody knows what the Communist society will
be like, but we do know that the advent of the proletariat to
the rank of ruling class will be tantamount to the end of prehistory. Thus Marx takes his position both before and after
"human practice" is complete.

He is still following Hegel when he regards "human actions
and their results as the end toward which all beings and all
processes tend." Not that he holds human history to be the end
toward which the cosmos tends or Communism to be the conclusion toward which previous societies aspired. Marx, especially in the second part of his life, claimed to perceive a
strict determinism; but if one refers to Engels' dialectic of nature, it clearly appears that the levels of reality are arranged
according to a qualitative hierarchy. Similarly, the moments
of history are oriented toward the fulfillment of human nature
and the humanization of society, although this result has not
been willed by a mind, individual or collective, and has not
aroused in the consciences of men a desire which has finally
been satisfied.

The idea that history is creative of truth, although it has not
been conceived previously by anybody, does not constitute the
originality of Marx's philosophy. The idea that the collective
good may be the necessary albeit unintentional result of non-
virtuous conduct is common to the majority of modern political and economic thinkers. It is essential to the philosophy of

Machiavelli; it is the foundation of political economics. Liberals and classicists adopt it with no less conviction than Marxists. Both groups are a prey to "doctrinarisms," in spite of their fundamental opposition.

Indeed, both groups have revealed a mechanism of human behavior which should lead infallibly to prosperity and peace. The mechanism described by the liberals is that of prices: indeed, some of them do not hesitate to predict imminent servitude if state interventions jeopardize the functioning of this mechanism. This same mechanism of individual ownership and competition leads infallibly, according to Marx, to its own paralysis. Suffice it to add that the inevitable movement from one regime to another obeys a determinism comparable to that of equilibrium (according to the classicists) or that of progressive paralysis (according to the Marxists), and culminates in the dialectic of the self-destruction of capitalism.

Knowledge of the laws governing the functioning and transformation of capitalism permits Marxism to claim both the privileges of history already made and the obligations of history to be made. The future for a Marxist is significant in that it will bring the solution to the conflicts, and it is partially undetermined in that the moment and modalities of fulfillment are not foreseeable and are not, perhaps, rigorously determined.

Because of its ambiguity, this philosophy lends itself to many interpretations, some of which are not unacceptable to existentialists. The latter have no theory in the sense of a contemplative metaphysic embracing the whole of the cosmos and of humanity but, at least in the French school, they come close to the Marxists in their anthropological conceptions. They detest contemplative thought and the inner life, they see man essentially as the creature who works, who transforms his milieu and domesticates natural forces. Why would they not accept the Marxist vision of a historical development governed by an increase in the forces of production and culminating in the mastery of man over nature?

The Marxists and the existentialists come into conflict at the point where the tradition of Kierkegaard cannot be reconciled with that of Hegel: no social or economic regime can ever solve the enigma of history; individual destiny transcends collective life.[2] Individual consciousness always remains alone in the face of the mystery of life and death, however well organized may be the communal exploitation of the planet. The ultimate meaning of the human adventure is not given by the classless society, even if this society is inevitable.

The existentialists came to Marxism by way of the youthful writings of Marx. They adopted the dialectic of alienation and the reconquest of the self; the proletariat, totally alienated, realized a true intersubjectivity for this very reason. But at the same time they unwittingly fell prey to "doctrinarism": they referred particular societies to a universal model and, in a double arbitrary decree, they condemned certain societies and glorified others on the pretext that the latter represented the model, elevated to a supra-historical truth.

Marxism is by its very nature susceptible to doctrinarism. In calling the future revolution the end of prehistory, Marx confers on an action charged with the uncertainties peculiar to the human condition in a state of becoming, the dignity of a theoretical truth, the kind of truth that offers itself to the all-embracing view of the philosopher who contemplates cosmos and history at the end. In attributing to a particular class the function of abolishing the division into classes, he justifies the transfiguration of one group of men into the agents of the common salvation. The contradictions are inseparable from capitalism; only by violence can they be resolved. Thus we arrive at a strange philosophy in which peace will result from war pushed to its conclusion and the aggravation of the class struggle serves as a preface to the reconciliation or even the obliteration of classes.

This is not all. Marx's thinking was characterized by a radical error: the error of attributing all alienations to a single origin and of assuming that the end of economic alienation would

2 This doctrine, which is axiomatic for the author of *L'Etre et le néant*, cannot be attributed without reservation to the author of *La Phénoménologie de perception*.

result in the end of all alienation. In his *Introduction to the Critique of Hegel's Philosophy of Law*, Marx justly contrasted the freedom and equality the citizen enjoys in the political empyrean with the enslavement he suffers in bourgeois society (*bürgerliche Gesellschaft*), that is, in his professional activity. That the formal rights of the citizen are illusory for a proletarian trapped by a starvation wage is a profound truth. But this profound truth is transformed into a fatal illusion if one assumes that the liberation of labor implies political freedom and is identified with a certain status of ownership.

What curbed the potentialities of doctrinarism inherent in Marxism was the determinism of history as asserted by the thinkers of the Second International. As long as one allowed a correspondence between the development of the productive forces, the state of the relations of production, and the revolutionary capacity of the proletariat, action was still consistent with non-arbitrary circumstances, a predetermined development. An underdeveloped country could not arrive at socialism; socialism without democracy was not socialism.

French existentialists have not adopted this "objective determinism" of history. For this reason they have amplified the *doctrinarism* and multiplied those confusions between universal and particular to which all theoreticians are inclined and which are the major sin of political thought.

By doctrinarism I mean the attribution of universal value to a particular doctrine. Doctrinarism today is characterized by two modalities. In the first, the principles of the ideal order are identified with certain institutions. For example, one decrees that the democratic principle—governors are legitimate only if voluntarily accepted by the governed—is identical with free elections according to the British or French procedures, and instead of studying *hic et nunc* whether or in what form you can introduce elections in the Gold Coast or New Guinea, you dogmatically require that the electoral or parliamentary customs of a country be reproduced everywhere without regard for circumstances of time or place.

This type of doctrinarism involves two errors: the democratic principle of consent is exalted to the single principle of political order, and the institutional expression in *one* civilization—the electoral and parliamentary institutions of the West—is mistaken for the principle itself and receives a validity equal to this principle.

The second modality of doctrinarism is the historicist modality. The ideal order of the city depends less on the reason or will of men than on the necessary development of history. The movement of ideas and events will spontaneously realize the human community. Now, the philosopher can assert this providential character of history only if he knows or divines the distinguishing traits of the regime which will constitute its end. But how is one to know that the next phase of history will be its end if it is only in retrospect that one becomes aware of historical truth? Or again, by what right can one predict the imminent completion of history if by definition the future is unforeseeable? This contradiction is mitigated, if not eliminated, in the philosophy of Hegel because of the circularity of the system: the fact that the end refers back to the beginning and that at the end the contradictions that have set the system in motion are resolved gives sense, if not substantiation, to the completion of history.

A vulgarization of Hegelian themes aggravates the doctrinarism implicit in this way of thinking. If the end of history is identified with the universal and homogeneous state, there is a risk that the result will be the negation of particularities, of the rights of collectivities. The economic and political regime, arbitrarily likened to the universal and homogeneous state, is invested with a universal dignity. The wisdom of Montesquieu —the same laws are not good everywhere—disappears, because the historical contingency is subordinated to the alleged logic of evolution. Such a philosophy of history, which I propose to call *historicist doctrinarism,* seems to contradict itself. Insofar as it is historicist, it takes account of the diversity of customs, political regimes, and values; it denies that one can determine a political truth a priori or relate customs to a norm that is valid for all times and all places. But at the same time it assumes that the historical contingency obeys a rational law and automatically arrives at the solution to the problems that confront humanity.

The Western democracies tend toward a moralistic doctrinarism which is limited to politics. Governments are worthy to the degree that they illustrate or approximate the only regime that corresponds to the ideal, democracy (free elections and representative institutions), a doctrinarism which usually is not so much explicitly stated as vaguely felt and which is accompanied by the explicit rejection of any hierarchy of values between the way of life of the Hottentots and the Pygmies and that of the Americans or French of today. Soviet doctrinarism is historicist: it is the historical dialectic which will bring about the ideal regime, elevated to universal acceptance.

Both forms of doctrinarism implicitly retain a philosophy of progress: At a certain moment in history man has been capable of grasping the truth for himself and of mastering natural forces. Moralism does not rigorously fix the stages of this discovery and this mastery, whereas historicism specifies their order even if it is sometimes forced to skip one stage or add another. Moralism does not seek the conditions indispensable to this absolute, always possible moment. Historicism, in theory, makes the beneficent rupture depend upon circumstances, but in practice both doctrinarisms are inspired by the same confidence in the power of the human will and the unlimited resources of technology.

The doctrinarism of the existentialists is particularly revealing. It presents, exaggerated to the point of caricature, the intellectual errors which paralyze political thought. The existentialists begin with an almost nihilistic denial of all human or social constancy, only to end with a dogmatic affirmation of "a single truth" in an area where the truth cannot be single. The critique of dogmatism is at the same time a critique of nihilism. At least, such was the objective of *The Opium of the Intellectuals,* although people chose to see it as only a testimony to skepticism.

Economic Progress and Political Constancy

Many critics, even some of those who were sympathetic to the book, criticized *The Opium of the Intellectuals* for being negative, for abounding in refutations without providing anything constructive. I earned this reproach by writing the last sentence—"Let us all pray for the coming of the skeptics if they will put an end to fanaticism"— although the whole of the last page means exactly the opposite of what hurried readers found there. As a matter of fact, I expressed the fear, not the hope, that the loss of so-called absolute truths might incline intellectuals toward skepticism: "Yet man, who does not expect a miraculous change either from revolution or from reform, is not obliged to resign himself to the unjustifiable. He does not give his soul to an abstract humanity, a tyrannical party, an absurd scholasticism, because he loves people, participates in living communities, respects the truth."

Many of the writings that are termed "constructive" are just as futile as plans for a universal state or a new organization of business. The term "constructive" is applied even to projects that are unrealizable, and the term "negative" to analyses which tend to delimit what is possible and to form political judgment—a judgment which is essentially historical in nature and which must focus on the real or set itself an attainable objective. One is sometimes tempted to invert the hierarchy of values and to take the term "negative" as a compliment.

The only criticism that would deserve to be classified as negative would be one which, while dispelling illusions, did not help to discover or judge the present or permanent reality.

Before 1917, no Marxist[3] believed a socialist revolution to be possible in a country where the industrial proletariat numbered only three million workers and represented only a paltry minority. Of course it is always possible to reconcile an inter-

[3] One can find passages in which Marx foresaw that the revolution would break out in Russia, whose social and political structure was more fragile than that of the West. But this idea is difficult to reconcile with the classic theory in the Introduction to the *Contribution to the Critique of Political Economy*.

pretation with reality by introducing a supplementary hypothesis: Russia, because economic development had been retarded there, constituted the weakest link in the capitalist chain; the industry there was concentrated, largely financed by foreign capital, and for this reason it aroused greater rebelliousness in the masses than the national industry of the countries of western Europe, although it had arrived at a later phase.

All these hypotheses do not explain away certain major facts which we would not need to recall if certain left-wing intellectuals did not go out of their way to forget them: The revolutions which call themselves Marxist have succeeded only in countries where the development typical of capitalism has not occurred; the strength of the Communist parties in the West is in inverse ratio to the development of capitalism; it is not the capitalist dynamism which swells the ranks of the revolutionary parties in France or Italy, but the paralysis of this dynamism.

From these major facts two conclusions may immediately be drawn. The first of these, which is theoretical, involves one of the classic versions of historical materialism, which is found in the Introduction to the *Contribution to the Critique of Political Economy*. It is manifestly false that humanity sets itself only problems that it is capable of solving, false that the relations of production correspond to the development of the forces of production, false that the state of ownership corresponds to the state of the forces of production, false that the movement of the economy is autonomous or obeys a determinism of its own. The rise of the Bolshevik party preceded the expansion of the proletariat and of capitalism, due to exceptional circumstances (war, difficulties of food control, the collapse of the traditional regime). The Bolshevik party was able to seize the power and so prove that the form of the state and the conceptions of the governors could determine, as well as reflect, the economic organization.

The second conclusion, which is historical, is that there is no parallelism or correspondence between the development of the forces of production and the shift from capitalism to socialism. One cannot dogmatically decree that a country with a so-called capitalist regime (individual ownership of the means of production, mechanisms of the market) will not someday arrive at a so-called socialist regime (collective ownership, curtailment or elimination of the mechanisms of the market). In this sense a non-Stalinist Marxist could say that General Motors is no longer an example of individual ownership since the shares are divided among hundreds of thousands of persons. One would need only subordinate the board of directors to the state or to a mixed committee of shareholders, workers, and employees to arrive at a state which certain Marxists would not hesitate to call socialist. Similar observations might be made in regard to the mechanisms of the market, whose sphere of influence is shrinking, and the planned economy, which is gradually gaining.

However valid these conclusions may be in the long run, if by socialism one means the Soviet regime and by capitalism the regime of the Western countries, the present rivalry between socialism and capitalism has nothing in common with the struggle between the future and the past, between two stages in the development of industrial society. For the moment we are witnessing a rivalry between two methods of industrialization, and there is no reason why the most effective way of running the American economy must necessarily be the best way of initiating or accelerating industrialization in India or China.

In other words, there is a Marxist critique of the Stalinist interpretation of the world situation. If one refers to the phases of economic growth, a planned economy of the Soviet type is a crude technique for catching up with more advanced countries at the price of imposing sacrifices on populations even more severe than those imposed by industrialization in western Europe during the first half of the nineteenth century.

A Marxist critique of this kind which adopted the primacy of the forces of production would arrange the various economic regimes in an order which would culminate in the regime of the Western type, and in which the liberalism of nineteenth-century Europe and the sovietism of the twentieth century would be two modalities of an outmoded stage. Even if one does not subscribe to this critique, the fact remains that one cannot discuss a socialism which has built an enormous industry by reducing the standard of living of the masses and a capitalism which has raised the standard of living, reduced working hours, and permitted the consolidation of labor unions, as if these were the same realities that Marx considered a century ago or that he anticipated according to a system which has since been refuted by events.

We must therefore distinguish the choice between socialism and capitalism from the choice between sovietism and a society of the Western type, and raise separately the question of reforms to be introduced to Western societies characterized by rapid expansion (United States), societies characterized by slower expansion (France), and the various underdeveloped societies. To force the Chinese, Russian, North Korean, and Czech regimes into the same category of socialism, and the French, American, Egyptian, and Indian regimes into the same category of capitalism, is to be sure of understanding nothing and confusing everything. Reference to the theory of economic growth and the phases of growth at least enables one to avoid an error which we whom old-timers call revolutionaries have been denouncing for ten years and which Merleau-Ponty condemns today: the error of defining the Soviet Union by public enterprise and the United States by free enterprise.

In criticizing this historical error we thereby eliminate the philosophical error which consisted in attributing a suprahistoric value to the Marxist dialectic of alienation, as identified with the capitalism-socialism dialectic. Not that there is not a suprahistorical truth in the dialectic of alienation. Man creates institutions and loses himself in his creations. The challenging of institutions by man, who feels a stranger to himself in his own existence, is the source of the historical movement. The origin of doctrinarism is the implicit or explicit assumption that economic alienation is the primary cause of all alienations and that individual ownership of the means of production the primary cause of all economic alienation. Once this monism has been eliminated one can proceed to a reasonable comparison of the economic, social, and political advantages and disadvantages of the various regimes in themselves and according to the phases of growth.

The two economic values most commonly invoked in our time are increase of the gross national product and equalitarian distribution of income. It is not certain that a concern for increase inspires the same measures as a concern for equality. Nor has it been proved that industrial societies are capable of the same measure of equalization of income at various phases of their development. It is possible that the broadening of the salary range is favorable to productivity. Generally speaking, one can say that the two objectives—wealth and equalitarian justice—are not contradictory, since the facts suggest a reduction of inequalities with an increase of wealth. But at a given moment these two points of reference may compel one not to a radical choice, but to an ambiguous compromise.

However, the two criteria which we have just indicated are not the only ones. Limitation of the powers vested in the administrators of collective labor seems consistent with a fundamental requirement of a political nature. But the rigor of discipline and the authority of the leaders may be favorable to productivity. A comparison of the yield from private ownership and collective ownership, from public ownership where an absolute power reigns and democratized public ownership, may reveal contradictions between efficiency and a human ideal.

This way of raising the problems is imposed by a double critique: a sociological critique of a causal monism in which a *single* element (regime of ownership, a procedure for the establishment of equilibrium) determines the principle traits of an economic regime, and a philosophical critique of the use to which the existentialists have put the dialectic of alienation, a dialectic which acquires concrete value in the sociological translation which Marx gave it but which without this translation remains formal and applicable to all regimes.

This plurality of considerations does not prevent one from

grasping wholes, from comprehending a political and economic regime such as the Soviet regime or the American regime in its unity or essence. This procedure, however precarious, is scientifically legitimate and politically inevitable. It must be prefaced by an analysis which has revealed the traits common to all regimes and the advantages or disadvantages peculiar to each.

Every modern economic regime is characterized by factory workers, and the proportion of skilled workers to non-skilled workers depends more on technology than on the state of ownership. The factory workers will be embedded in a collective organization of administration and labor without being capable of grasping fully the meaning of the tasks that are entrusted to them. The condition of the workers nevertheless varies greatly according to size of salaries, breadth of salary range, relations within the factory or business, relations between labor unions and leaders, private or public, and according to their sense of participation or alienation, a sense that is partially determined by the ideology to which the workers subscribe and the idea they have of the society. To declare flatly that a worker in a capitalist factory in France or the United States is by definition exploited and that a worker in a Soviet factory is not, is not an example of synthetic thought, it is pure nonsense. It is merely a convenient way of substituting verbal gymnastics for a painstaking investigation of reality.

From Criticism to Reasonable Action

Politics is action: political theory is either the comprehension of action crystallized in events or the determination of what action is possible or advisable in a given situation. Since to my way of thinking completed action has not obeyed laws or a dialectic, I cannot offer the equivalent of the Marxist doctrine in which past and future, knowledge and practice are united in a single system. Since the present situation of the world, considered in the context of an economic interpretation, gives rise to different problems in underdeveloped countries, Western countries of retarded growth, and Western countries of accelerated growth,[4] the true doctrine can only be one which shows the diversity of solutions.

To be sure, I have not explicitly indicated either the objectives to be aimed at or the hierarchy to be established among the objectives—I have deliberately refrained from discussing objectives—but these, in fact, are imperatively suggested by modern civilization. They are the objectives of the left, henceforth victorious—a left which runs the risk of being defeated by its own victory. I have not challenged the values of the left; one need only define clearly *all* of these values to reveal their possible contradiction and consequently the partial truth of the men and doctrines of the right.

The major fact of our age is neither socialism, nor capitalism, nor the intervention of the state, nor free enterprise: it is the monstrous development of technology and industry, of which the massive concentrations of workers in Detroit, Billancourt, Moscow, and Coventry are the consequence and symbol. Industrial society is the genus of which Soviet and Western societies are the species.

No nation and no party rejects or can consciously reject industrial civilization, which is the foundation not only of the living standard of the masses, but of military strength. It is conceivable that the ruling classes of certain Islamic or Asiatic countries would tolerate the poverty of their populations (even with Western technology, they cannot be sure of remedying this poverty if the birth rate remains too high) ; they would not tolerate a position of subservience to which they would be condemned by the absence of industry. In the native land of Gandhi the rulers are impressed by the Soviet example, which is an example of power much more than an example of abundance.

The imperative of economic progress forces right-wing thinkers to accept the instability of the conditions of existence from one generation to another.[5] This same imperative obliges left-

4 It goes without saying that these three types of countries are not the only ones: I am presenting a simplified typology.

5 It would be worth reflecting on the significance of conservatism in an economically progressive society.

wing thinkers to consider the compatibility or incompatibility of their various ends.

It has been established that the standard of living of the workers depends more on the productivity of work than on the form of ownership of businesses, that the distribution of income is not necessarily less equitable under a regime of private ownership and competition than under a regime of planned economy. If the two major objectives of the left in the economic realm are growth and fair distribution, experimental proof exists to the effect that public ownership and planned economy are not necessary means. Socialist doctrinarism is born of a devotion to anachronistic ideologies. The critique of myths leads directly not to a choice, but to a reasonable consideration of the regimes in which nations have to live.

But why should I have brought up the matter of choice? Neither the Americans nor the British nor the French nor the Soviets have to choose from among different regimes. The Americans and the British are satisfied with their regime and will modify it in accordance with events. If a crisis should arise they will not hesitate to intervene, even if it becomes necessary to move, without admitting it or while insisting on the contrary, toward a kind of planned economy. One need only show that the economic objectives of the left may be attained within the context of the Western regimes to dispel the prestige of the revolutionary mythology and encourage men to use reason to solve problems which are more technological than ideological.

The case of France is unusual. It would seem that the French economy suffers from an insufficiency of dynamism. Her geographical situation and the sentiments of the people rule out the imitation or importation of the Soviet regime, not to speak of the repugnance that would be felt by the vast majority of Frenchmen (including most of those who vote for the Communist party) for Soviet methods as soon as they had any direct experience of them. So criticism, by dispelling nostalgia for the beneficial upheaval, clears the way for the effort of construction.

There is not so much difference, in France, between a so-called leftist economist like Mr. Sauvy and a so-called rightist economist like myself. To be sure, Mr. Sauvy sometimes suggests that the feudal powers are the principal persons responsible for stagnation. He is not unaware that resistance to change comes from the small at least as much as from the great and that workers' unions or unions of civil servants or agricultural producers are just as given to Malthusianism as employers' unions. He sometimes promotes the legend of an expansionist left against a Malthusian right, although he has shown better than anyone to what a degree the government of the Popular Front of 1936 had been Malthusian out of ignorance.

To me loyalty to one party has never been a decision of fundamental importance. To join the Communist party is to accept a theory of the world and of history. To join the Socialist party or the MRP (*Mouvement républicain populaire*) is to demonstrate one's loyalty to or at least sympathy for a representation of society, a spiritual family. I do not believe in the validity of a system comparable to that of the Communists; I feel detached from the preferences or *Weltanschauung* of the left or the right, the socialists or radicals, the MRP or the independents. According to the circumstances I am in agreement or disagreement with the action of a given movement or a given party. In 1941 or 1942 I disapproved of the passion with which the Gaullists, from the outside, denounced the "treason" of Vichy. In 1947 I favored a revision of the Constitution or of constitutional procedure which the *Rassemblement du peuple français* professed to want. When the attempt of the RPF failed, the social republicans aggravated the faults of the regime, and I could neither associate myself with their action nor keep silent about its disastrous consequences. Perhaps such an attitude is contrary to the morality (or immorality) of political action; it is not contrary to the obligations of the writer.

If my criticisms seem to be directed primarily against the left, the fault may lie with the desire which motivates me to convince my friends. The fault also lies with the attitude adopted by the majority of leftists today, an attitude which I see as a betrayal of the "eternal" left.

The left came out of the movement of the Enlightenment.

It places intellectual freedom above all else, it wants to tear down all Bastilles, it aspires to the simultaneous flowering of wealth, through the exploitation of natural resources, and justice, through the decline of superstition and the reign of Reason. That prejudice in favor of the tyranny of a single party which elevates a pseudo-rationalist superstition into an official ideology is, in my opinion, the shame of the intellectuals of the left. Not only are they sacrificing the best part of the legacy of the Enlightenment—respect for reason, liberalism—but they are sacrificing it in an age when there is no reason for the sacrifice, at least in the West, since economic expansion in no sense requires the suppression of parliaments, parties, or the free discussion of ideas.

Here again, the criticism of myth has an immediate positive function. How have the intellectuals been drawn into this denial?[6] Through the *monist* error: ultimately, the Marxist ignores politics; he decrees that the economically dominant class is by definition in possession of the power. The arrival of the proletariat to the rank of ruling class will be tantamount to the liberation of the masses. Having traced the origin of economic alienation to private ownership of the instruments of production, we arrive at the ludicrous conclusion that public ownership of the instruments of production and the omnipotence of one party are tantamount to the classless society, by a series of verbal equivalences (power of the party = power of the proletariat = abolition of private ownership = abolition of classes = human liberation).

Economic expansion, whether pursued by the Soviet method or the Western method, never guarantees a respect for political values. The increase of total wealth or even the reduction of economic inequalities implies neither the safeguarding of personal or intellectual freedom nor the maintaining of representative institutions. Indeed, as Tocqueville and Burckhardt saw

[6] I shall omit the psychological reasons, conscious or unconscious, to which I alluded in *The Opium of the Intellectuals* and which provoked so much criticism. An intellectual of the left has the right to regard all businessmen and all right-wing writers as bigots or cynics. It is high treason to suggest that "interests" are not confined to one side, and Mr. Duverger does not hesitate to draw an idealized portrait of the intellectual whose sole concern is to defend the oppressed and combat injustice. The picture is edifying.

clearly a century ago, societies without an aristocracy, motivated by the spirit of commerce and the boundless desire for wealth, are susceptible to the conformist tyranny of majorities and the concentration of power in a monstrous state. Whatever tensions may be created by the retardation of economic progress in France, the most difficult task from a long-range historical point of view is not to assure the increase of collective resources, but to avoid falling into the tyranny of mass societies.

I do not oppose those leftist intellectuals who demand the acceleration of economic growth in France. Although I am probably more aware than they are of the cost of growth, I am nevertheless in agreement with them in principle, as long as they are not fascinated by the Soviet model. I do condemn them for the partiality that prompts them always to take sides against the Westerners: though ready to accept Communism in the underdeveloped countries to promote industrialization, they nevertheless remain hostile to the United States, which can give lessons in industrialization to all of us. When it is a question of the Soviet Union, economic progress justifies the destruction of national independence in Asia or even in Europe. When it is a question of European colonies, the right of peoples to self-determination is invoked in all its rigor. The semi-violent repression practiced by the Westerners in Cyprus or Africa is denounced ruthlessly, while the radical repression in the Soviet Union, with transfers of populations, is ignored or pardoned. The democratic freedoms are invoked against the democratic governments of the West, but their disappearance is excused when it is the work of a regime that calls itself proletarian.

Skepticism and Faith

Have I fully explained why *The Opium of the Intellectuals* is regarded as a negative book? Certainly not, and I see other reasons myself.

Many readers are irritated by what one of my adversaries at the *Centre des Intellectuels catholiques* has called "my dramatic dryness." I must confess to an extreme repugnance to reply to this type of argument. Those who let it be known that their own sentiments are noble and those of their adversaries selfish or base strike me as exhibitionists. I have never considered that there was any merit or difficulty in suffering or that sympathy for the misery of others was the prerogative of those who write for *Le Monde, Les Temps modernes, L'Esprit,* or *La Vie intellectuelle.* Political analysis gains by divesting itself of all sentimentality. Lucidity demands effort: passion automatically goes at a gallop.

I reproach Merleau-Ponty, to whom I feel so close, for having written against Sartre that "one doesn't get rid of poverty simply by hailing the revolution from afar." Of course one does not get rid of it so cheaply, but how are we privileged persons to discharge our debt? All my life I have only known one person whom the misery of others prevented from living: Simone Weil. She followed her path and ended in quest of sainthood. We whom the misery of men does not prevent from living—at least let it not prevent us from thinking. Let us not believe ourselves obliged to talk nonsense to bear witness to our noble sentiments.

Also, I refuse to pass those hasty judgments to which so many of my adversaries and even friends invite me. I refuse to say, with Mr. Duverger, that "the left is the party of the weak, the oppressed and the victims," for that party, the party of Simone Weil, is neither to the right nor to the left; it is eternally on the side of the vanquished, and as everybody knows, Mr. Duverger does not belong to it. I refuse to say that "at the present time Marxism provides the only comprehensive theory of social injustice," for in that case the biologists would have to say that Darwinism as expounded by Darwin provides the only comprehensive theory of the evolution of the species. I refuse to denounce capitalism as such, or the bourgeoisie as such, to hold the "feudal lords" (which ones?) responsible for the errors committed in France over the past fifty years. Every society has a ruling class, and the party which is volunteering today to take over brings with it a society worse than the existing one. I consent to denounce social injustices but not social injustice itself, of which private ownership is alleged to be the major cause and Marxism the theory.

I am quite aware that Etienne Borne, who only wishes me well, reproaches me in a friendly way for "deploying an immense talent in order to explain with irrefutable reasons why things cannot be otherwise than what they are." It is true that I argue against utopianism more often than against conservatism. In France at the present time, the criticism of ideologies is one way of hastening reforms. On the level of philosophy, not of the daily paper, Etienne Borne as well as Father Leblond reproach me for not indicating in the foreseeable future the reconciliation of values which are temporarily incompatible. A strange reproach coming from Catholics who believe the world to be corrupted by sin!

It seems to me essential to reveal the plurality of considerations on which political or economic action must depend. I do not regard this plurality as incoherent. In the economic realm the concern for production and the concern for equitable distribution are not in the long run either contradictory or concordant. The reconciliation of justice with growth requires a compromise between equality and the adjustment of retribution to merit. The economic objective of a better living standard often comes into conflict with the political objective of power.

In the political realm it seems to me that the fundamental problem is to reconcile the participation of all men in the community with the diversity of tasks. Men have sought the solution to this antinomy in two ways. The first way is to proclaim the social and political equality of individuals in spite of the prestige of the functions performed by each. No doubt modern societies are the only ones to have extended universally the principle of equality which the ancient city states limited to citizens alone and which even the Roman Empire did not extend either to slaves or to all conquered peoples. But the more democracy tries to restore to complex societies that economic and social equality which small, non-literate populations maintained with difficulty, the more apparent becomes the contrast between justice and reality. Democratic societies and Soviet societies are doomed, albeit to different degrees, to hypocrisy, because the weight of things does not permit them to effectively realize their ideal.

The second solution consists in sanctioning the inequality of conditions and rendering it acceptable by convincing all non-privileged persons that the hierarchy reflects a higher cosmic or religious order and that it does not impair the dignity or opportunity of the individual. The caste system is the extreme form of the unequalitarian solution which has, at its worst, given rise to horrors, but whose principle was not inherently hateful. Or at least if the unequalitarian solution is inherently imperfect, the other solution is too, at least as long as circumstances do not make it possible to realize it effectively.

Indeed, the religion of salvation has, throughout history, oscillated between two extremes. Either it has sanctioned or accepted the temporal inequalities by devaluating them: in comparison to the sole essential, the salvation of the soul, what importance have the things of this world, wealth and power? Or else it has denounced social and economic inequalities in the name of evangelical truth and solemnly called upon men to reorganize institutions in accordance with the precepts of Christ and the Church. Each of these two attitudes involves a danger to the authenticity of religion. The first runs the risk of leading to a kind of quietism, a complacent acceptance of injustices, and even the sanctification of the established order. The second, carried to its conclusion, would sustain the revolutionary impulse, since societies have, up to the present, been so incapable of giving their citizens that equality of condition or opportunity which is solemnly granted to souls.

The Christian socialists (and by inspiration, the progressists belong to this tradition) often have the conviction that they alone are capable of saving the Church from compromising itself with the established injustice, that they and they alone are faithful to the teachings of Christ. Churches, even churches of salvation, never entirely avoid relapsing into what Bergson called static religion. They are inclined to justify the powers which accord them a monopoly (or, in our time, certain privileges) in the realm of the administration of sacraments or the education of the young. The Christian, whose opinions are politically conservative, and the clergy, concerned about schools or convents, tend, in order to excuse a lack of concern for social inequalities, to invoke the idea that the real match is not played in the political arena. At the other extreme the progressist carries historical hope—i.e., temporal hope—as far as it will go.

I shall refrain from choosing between these two attitudes: either, in its authentic expression, may legitimately call itself Christian. Perhaps the most profoundly Christian citizen would be one who experienced at every moment the tension between these two exigencies. He would never have the sense of having done enough for human justice, and yet he would feel that the results of this tireless effort were negligible and must appear as such in comparison with the only thing really at stake. He would be neither resigned to human misery nor forgetful of sin.

In our day in France the pendulum is swinging toward evangelical socialism, at least in the intellectual Catholic circles of the capital. The "hierarchy" is criticized for taking an exaggerated interest in the schools and for compromising itself with the "established disorder," to quote E. Mounier, in a vain effort to collect a few subsidies from the state. I have not taken sides in this debate, and there was no reason why I should. It makes no difference to me whether the Catholics vote for the left or for the right. What interests me is the fact that some Catholics are so attracted by the parties that promise the kingdom of God on earth that they forgive them for persecutions inflicted on Christians in China and eastern Europe.

I was quite surprised, at the *Centre des Intellectuels catholiques,* to hear a Jesuit father, as far as possible from progressism, present the anticipation of the kingdom of God on earth as a hope, if not a belief, that was necessary. What is the definition of this kingdom of God? I am astonished at the facility with which Catholic thinkers are adopting the optimism of the age of Enlightenment, amplified and vulgarized by Marxism. The attempt to outflank the Communists on the left strikes me as politically futile and, in terms of doctrine, if not of dogma, questionable. Besides, this technological optimism belongs to the avant-garde of yesterday rather than to that of today.

I have not even criticized this optimism as such; I have confined myself to tracing the steps by which one passes from the classless society—the materialist version of the kingdom of God on earth—to a theory of historical evolution, to one class, then to one party as the agent of salvation.

Finally, the stages of profane history—the succession of social regimes—are confused with the moments of sacred history, the dialogue of men (and of each man) with God. It is necessary and easy to mark the separation between these two histories and to remember that anyone who believes totally in the first ceases for that very reason to believe in the second.

My friend Father Dubarle, in an intelligent article, begins by agreeing with me so closely that he considers the point too obvious to require proof. "Surely, then, history, the real and concrete history which presents itself at the level of human experience and reason, is not that secular substitute for divinity which has fascinated so many contemporary minds with its dream. All these things are very well said, and one feels, moreover, when one reflects, a certain surprise (a surprise which is shared by Mr. Aron) to find that there is such a need for them to be said in our day. . . ." Then he suggests by means of subtle questions that the rigorous separations between temporal and eternal, profane and sacred may provide more apparent clarity than real light. I shall try, however, to reply to these questions which I am not sure I really understand.

"A Christian," he writes, "would therefore ask Mr. Aron whether he can accept the idea that a sermon about eternity tries also to confer, albeit in a subordinate and relative fashion, a humanly important significance to the temporal history of the human race." I have never dreamed of refusing "a humanly important significance to the temporal history of the human race." Not being a believer in the ordinary sense of the term, how could I have denied this importance without falling into out-and-out nihilism? The discussion does not concern "the importance of the temporal history"; the discussion concerns the truth of an interpretation of history that shows humanity advancing toward the classless society, with one class and one party playing the role of savior in this adventure. Once this mythology has been eliminated, temporal history remains important, but it ceases to obey either a pre-established determinism or a dialectic; it imposes on men tasks that are constantly being renewed and fundamentally permanent. Never will men finish subjecting the weight of institutions to the desire for justice.

Let us not go into the problem of clericalism or the role of the church in societies that reject a state religion: I have not dealt with this problem, to which Father Dubarle for some reason alludes. In twentieth-century France the Church accepts the fact that the state declares religion to be a "private affair." It no longer demands that the state impose by force the universal truth to which it continues, legitimately from its point of view, to lay claim; it consents to civic and political equality being accorded to nonbelievers. I do not believe that Father Dubarle is any less a partisan of secularity than myself.

Secularity does not reduce the Church to the administration of the sacraments or condemn her to silence in the realm of politics or economics. The Church wants to imbue the organization of the City with the Christian spirit. In this sense all Christians, and not progressist Christians alone, want to "introduce the eternal into the temporal." But they do not all think that this introduction leads, according to a deterministic or dialectical order, to the kingdom of God on earth. But when I deny that the evolution is orderly or that the vision is ever total, I am immediately suspected of denying all significance to history and all commerce between the eternal and the temporal. Strange misunderstanding, or rather, one that reveals so much! Anyone who has understood the nature of men and societies knows that "Christianity" involves a secular effort and the acceptance of a role in the game of history. He also knows that this game is never entirely won, or in any case that profane history, economic or social history, will have no final fulfillment. Neither the Christian nor the rationalist therefore turns away from the temporal drama, for even if they know nothing about the future they do know something about the principles of a human society. If so many Catholics are afraid to renounce the historical dialectic it is because they too have lost their principles and, like the existentialists, look to myths for the certainties they lack.

The progressist Christians play among believers a role analogous to that of the existentialists among unbelievers. The latter incorporate fragments of Marxism into a philosophy of extreme individualism and quasi-nihilism because, denying any permanence to human nature, they oscillate between a lawless voluntarism and a doctrinarism based on myths. The progressist Christians refuse to judge regimes according to the conditions imposed on churches and are ready to attribute an almost sacred value to an economic technique, the class struggle, or a method of action. When I denounce the conversion of Kierkegaard's descendants to doctrinarism or the oscillation of the progressists between "revolutionarism" toward the liberal societies and "secular clericalism" favoring the Communist societies, I am accused of skepticism, as if my skepticism were aimed at authentic faith when in fact it is aimed at schemes, models, and utopias.

This skepticism is useful or harmful according to whether fanaticism or indifference is more to be feared; in any case it is philosophically necessary insofar as it will put an end to the ravages of abstract passions and bring men back to the elementary distinction between principles and judgments based on expediency. For want of principles both existentialists and progressist Christians count on a class or a historical dialectic to provide them with conviction. Dogmatic when they should be cautious, the existentialists have begun by denying what they should have affirmed. They have no use for prudence, "the god of this world below"; they invest the historical movement with reason after having divested it of man. The progressists attribute to Revolution that sacred quality which they are afraid of no longer finding in the life of the Church and the adventures of souls.

Is it, then, so difficult to see that I have less against fanaticism than I have against skepticism, which is its ultimate origin?

THIRD DIALOGUE
La Critique
de la raison dialectique
a Century After
the Founding of the
First International

The Impact of Marxism
in the Twentieth Century*

The word "impact" is difficult to translate (or to define, if one regards it as French). Does it mean influence, shock, challenge? Probably the English word suggests all these meanings—and in doing so indicates the immensity of the ground we should have to cover if we had the absurd ambition to try, in a single essay, to answer the question, or rather the multiple questions, posed by the title at the top of this page.

The term "Marxism," moreover, is hardly less equivocal than "impact." Indeed, Marxism may denote: (1) the ideas of Marx himself, as reconstructed by the historian who seeks to understand them in relation to the man and his times; (2) the ideas of Marx as interpreted by various "Marxist" schools in relation to their own times, their own problems, their own goals; (3) the social movements, the parties in opposition, and the parties in power that claim to be acting or governing in accordance with Marxist ideas. Between the second and third definitions, i.e., between the *ideas* that spokesmen for Marxist movements attribute to Marx and the movements themselves, there is necessarily a dialectical relationship. Every movement creates its own Marxism, or reads the writings of Marx in its own way, just as every religious sect has its own way of reading Holy Writ, although of course the texts themselves influence the being and

* This article was written in the fall of 1964 on the occasion of a conference organized by the Hoover Institute of Stanford University to commemorate the hundredth anniversary of the founding of the First International.

consciousness of the reader, and hence the way he reads them.

Even if we hold to the first definition, the term Marxism is still not free from ambiguity. Equally objective historians do not necessarily come to the same general conclusions—for two main reasons, both of which stem from the peculiar nature of Marxism. First, the historian hesitates between theories that are often crude and historical and sociological analyses that are rich and subtle. In every one of his historical studies Marx discerned a number of classes, even though on the theoretical level he asserted that capitalist society tends to polarize into two classes, the proletariat and the bourgeoisie. Similarly, in his historical studies, he did in fact recognize and take note of the role played by the state, by parties, even by individual men, while in theory the state is only a tool in the service of the economically dominant class. Finally, certain basic concepts—"the relations of production," "infrastructure," "superstructure," "in the final analysis"—seem destined to remain the source of endless controversy, of a theological rather than scientific nature.

The linking of *materialism* and *the dialectic* and the differences in style and vocabulary between the so-called youthful writings (before the *Poverty of Philosophy* and the *Communist Manifesto*) and those of the mature period inevitably promote controversy. There are, to put it simply, two philosophical methods of interpreting Marxism: one in which dialectic and Hegelian influence dominate, the other in which materialism dominates. Either the laws of the dialectic are an objective description of natural (cosmic, theological, biological, human) development, or else the dialectic is related to the wellspring of human action—history is dialectical because men deny reality and reach toward a future that, when it becomes objective reality, is in turn denied by later generations. These two philosophical methods are not fundamentally incompatible; the Hegelianized Marx of Georg Lukács is still a materialist—at least in the sense that the contradictions of capitalism, and the objective dialectic they give rise to, still play a central role in *History and Class Consciousness*. Even so, the materialism propounded by Lenin in his book *Materialism and Empirio-Criti-*

cism and the materialism of the young Lukács, or of the Sartre of *La Critique de la raison dialectique,* have hardly anything in common but the name.

This duality of philosophical interpretation was deepened, renewed, brought up to date, if you will, by the publication some thirty years ago (in 1932) of all Marx's early manuscripts, particularly the *Economic and Philosophic Manuscripts of 1844* and *The German Ideology* of 1845, the first antedating, the second postdating, the beginning of his collaboration with Engels. Although even by the time he wrote *The German Ideology* Marx repudiated the style and vocabulary of the 1844 manuscript; although he read and approved Engels' *Anti-Dühring,* which more than any other book by the two men is the source of classical Marxism and dialectical materialism; although the concept of alienation (*Entfremdung*) has almost disappeared in the great books of Marx's maturity—despite all this, an entire literature developed, first in Germany between 1919 and 1933, then in France after the Second World War, which tried to rethink Marxism in the light of manuscripts that Marx himself had never published.

This "Hegelianized" or "existentialized" Marx, though sometimes presented to us by historians of Marxism (Father Calvez, for example), is not independent of historical circumstance; he, too, fulfills an ideological function, like the materialist Marx of Lenin, Stalin, and Maurice Thorez. Of course, no social movement of any importance has made use of "existentialized Marxism," which is too difficult for the non-philosopher to understand, and which would strip Marxism of the double aura of *science* and *prescience.* In Sartrism scientific necessity is unintelligible, opaque to the mind, brute fact, not apodictic. But the intelligibility founded on freedom of constitutive dialectic would seem to imply that the future is unforeseeable. *History and Class Consciousness,* which is even more committed to the thesis of objective necessity and the foreseeability of social revolution, was never acceptable to Marxist-Leninist doctrinaires; it confines the primacy of economics to modern society, and, when all is said and done, undercuts the certainty of foresight by emphasizing the *efficacy* of class consciousness, the discovery by the historical subject of its historical calling.

To narrow our topic as much as possible, I shall put aside the first meaning of Marxism, i.e., Marxology, and give my attention to Marxist social movements and the doctrines that they propound. My remarks will center around the controversies between factions inside a given party, and between different parties that deem themselves equally loyal to Marx's thinking. Since these controversies arise from the clash between circumstance and doctrine, the title of this study might well be "Marxism at Grips with the Twentieth Century," or "On the Triumph of Marxism in a Century That Refutes Some of Its Main Ideas."

Marxists, like all true believers, are inclined to be quarrelsome, and the ambiguity of their faith reinforces this natural inclination. The theory of scientific socialism is first and foremost a *science of capitalism*. Marx analyzes the capitalist system and the way it functions in the light of a general concept of history and human society. He brings out its intrinsic contradictions, and he announces its inevitable destruction by the working class, which, as it becomes conscious of itself and of the exploitation of which it is the victim, organizes for revolutionary action. It is not impossible to extract from *Das Kapital* some indication of what a socialist economy should be like. But the fact remains that Marx, like all of his contemporaries, knew nothing of the problems of centralized planning, and that the pre-1917 Marxists gave much more thought to capitalism and its contradictions than to the role of money, prices, and interest in a socialist economy. If, as I believe, classical Marxism is essentially a theory of capitalism and thus of contemporary history, it is understandable that controversies between Marxists should be at once theoretical and practical: What action should be taken in circumstances unforeseen in the shared doctrine? What decision would most closely conform to the doctrine? How can today's decision or action be brought into line with a century-old doctrine, which, having become Holy Scripture, can be shaped to any purpose but cannot officially be revised? Is the socialism of the Soviet Union in agreement or in conflict with a doctrine that contains no description of the system to succeed capitalism?

It is hardly surprising that believers who were at the same time men of action have given contradictory answers to these questions.

The history of Marxist movements in the twentieth century is divided into four periods, and we have now entered the fifth. The first lasted until 1917: There was no Marxist state, only Marxist parties, all (or at least all the major ones) European. The Second International was dominated by the German Social Democrats. Neither Lenin nor Kautsky was aware that at the hour of decision they would both discover the precariousness of their agreement, the depth of their hostility.

October 1917: The victory of the Bolshevik party marked the first great schism inside the Marxist movement. The Second and the Third Internationals took separate roads, which were never to meet. The paths of reform and revolution were neither convergent nor parallel, but divergent. Pre-1917 classical Marxism might have had as its motto "Revolution through Reform." The post-1917 Marxists—gradually, even if they caught on slowly—lost their illusions; their slogan became "Reform or Revolution."

The second period ended with Stalin's rise to totalitarian power. From 1917 to 1930 the split between the two Internationals was completed, but doctrinal discussion among the factions of the Russian party had not been smothered. The Communist parties of the Third International were subject to the absolute authority of Moscow, but Moscow was not yet a monolith. The Bolshevik party had right and left wings, though the controversies that preceded industrialization were little known in the West at the time. Today, as we get further away from them, they are attracting new interest in the light of the events of the last thirty years.

From 1930 to 1953—a period we shall call, with Nikita Khrushchev, that of the cult of personality—Trotsky's famous prediction came true. The party took the place of the class, the

Central Committee that of the party, and finally the General Secretary that of the Central Committee. One man became the historical subject incarnate, and from then on the class could express its freedom only by passively submitting to an all-powerful ruler.

The fourth period opened with the death of the sovereign, or, if you prefer, with the Twentieth Congress of 1956. The party leaders, the comrades and heirs of Stalin, publicly confessed that they had been lying for years, out of fear; that socialist legality had been disregarded; that monstrous crimes had been committed; that innocent party workers by the tens of thousands had been shot or sent to concentration camps. And the truth about the concentration camps and about the Great Purge was, at least in part, admitted in the Soviet Union, and was spread unreservedly across the rest of the world. Simultaneously, the countries of eastern Europe regained limited autonomy. Under Khrushchev, Yugoslavia, which had been excommunicated during the preceding phase and subjected to an economic blockade for several years, once again became a Communist state in good standing—without, however, rejoining the bloc.

The quarrel between Moscow and Peking has opened a fifth phase, not only because of the historic importance of China, but because some of the basic tenets of Marxism-Leninism—especially those concerning relations among Communist states and between Communist and capitalist states (in other words peace, war, and imperialism)—have been called into question. Can the final struggle between the Communist camp and the capitalist camp take some form other than armed conflict? Won't a nonviolent transition to Communism become the rule, rather than the exception? Can a Communist country be imperialist? Can nationalism make enemies of two Communist countries? Would a world composed exclusively of Communist countries necessarily be a peaceful one? All these questions arise as soon as one considers the implications of the quarrel between Moscow and Peking.

In each one of these five periods, the Marxists have been engaged in impassioned controversies, which are summarized briefly below. We must then consider what interest these controversies have had for non-Marxists, and what influence they have exerted on the outside world.

The First Phase

The leading working-class parties of Continental Europe became more or less Marxist at the end of the last century. The British Labour party had never been so, and only a few intellectuals among its leaders had espoused Marxian beliefs—although they were never "converted" as the German and Russian Social Democrats were. Even on the Continent, commitment to the doctrine of the *Communist Manifesto* and *Das Kapital* varied in nature and scope from country to country. I have always had doubts about the authenticity of Jaurès's Marxism. Karl Kautsky's was dreadfully serious (*toternst,* as the Germans would say) .

The Second International, dominated by the German Social Democrats, was shaken by two public debates, on which attention was focused at the time. During the same period, the Russian Social Democrats were engaged in two debates that were no less impassioned, but that were known at the time only to the insiders (and most of the leaders of the Second International did not belong to the little group of insiders) . Subsequent events were to endow these debates with prophetic value.

One of the Second International's debates concerned the revisionism of Eduard Bernstein, the other what action the labor movement should take to prevent war. Although Bernstein was condemned by the German Social Democrats and the congresses of the International, today we think of him, far more than of his adversary Karl Kautsky, as the forebear and theoretician of twentieth-century democratic socialism. Because on the essential points—the evolution of the capitalist system, the influence of social reform—it is obviously Bernstein who after two world wars and the Great Depression has turned out to be right. Reforms wrested by trade unions or Socialist parties from capitalist societies do not lead to revolution. They transform capitalism, they humanize it, but they do not unsettle it.[1] Once this is apparent, either one must prevent the working class's progressive involvement in the private-property system and stake everything on an elite core of professional revolutionaries (Lenin's solution), or one must admit formulas such as Bernstein's: "The goal is the movement itself. . . . The sum total of the reforms *is* a revolution." At most, the Revolution that makes everyday action seem less prosaic can be seen as the myth in the eyes of the workers and party stalwarts. Bernstein's revisionism, like present-day democratic socialism, was founded on the assumption that the evolution of capitalism would be non-catastrophic, or, in other words, on the following two hypotheses: (1) the contradictions in capitalism will not keep intensifying, or, if they do, the ruling classes will be able to take the necessary steps to save the system; (2) the working class, or more broadly the masses, themselves are beneficiaries, and not victims, of the development of the forces of production.[2] If these two hypotheses are borne out (as they seemed to be before the First World War, and have seemed to be since the Second World War), reformism regularly tends to win out over revolutionary radicalism. Besides, Marxism is sufficiently flexible to stand warrant for a reformist doctrine.

In restrospect Kautsky was in an impossible position between Lenin and Bernstein, whose analyses of the situation had more in common than they cared to admit, but from which they drew exactly opposite conclusions. At the time Kautsky represented the center—and all its contradictions. The party workers were becoming too bourgeois not to denounce "Blanquism," and those working for a violent seizure of power, but they were insufficiently converted to democratic rhetoric to accept the theory underlying their practice. The Socialists were willing to act as though Bernstein were right, but they continued to think as though Kautsky were speaking the truth. In 1917 these two men found themselves in the same camp once more.

---

[1] At least when capitalism is defined as essentially private ownership of the means of production.

[2] Or, in non-Marxian terms, of economic growth.

The debates of the International on the war question had revealed a helplessness that was tragically confirmed by the events of July–August 1914. The largest of the European Socialist parties, the German Social Democrats, never believed they could prevent war by means of a general strike and had never intended to try. Whatever reason is given for this refusal —resignation to the inevitable course of history, justified by a determinist philosophy; hope that revolution would follow the war; patriotism, nationalism, or imperialism among sections of the working class and the Socialist party—the fact remains that the Second International had denounced capitalism in advance as responsible for any future war, but had been unable to agree on means to prevent that war. In August 1914 the German Social Democrats debated the advisability of voting for or against war credits, not the chances of a general strike or popular revolt. The situation in France was the same. The French workers, like the German workers, had a country to defend—the French against Germany, the Germans against Russia.

During this same period, the Russian Social Democrats, a minority party at the Second International, generated polemics and schisms by the dozen, amid the somewhat scornful indifference of their West European comrades. Today, of course, we know that the debates of the Russian Social Democrats prefigured later events: Was Lenin right to oppose the trade-unionist tendency of the working class if left to shift for itself by the creation of a party composed of professional revolutionaries and organized on the principle of "democratic centralism"? Or was Trotsky right to predict and denounce the substitution of the party for the class—and, ultimately, the substitution of the General Secretary for the party? Or were they both right at the same time, the one on the plane of effectiveness, the other on the nature of the system that a victorious Leninist party would establish? Furthermore, could a revolution in a country like Russia, still in the early stages of industrialization, become a socialist revolution without a transitional period of bourgeois democracy? Or, in more general terms, did all countries have to go through the same stages that western Europe had gone through? Finally—and this last question was not taken up again in the West until after the Second World War—did not a system of public ownership and state planning risk a return to what Marx called the Asiatic method of production instead of an advance to the superior method of socialism?

Of the two ideas on which Communism was based, Lenin conceived one (the elitist party of professional revolutionaries, organized on the principle of democratic centralism), Trotsky the other ("the weakest link in the chain"). Both concepts were indispensable for the transition from Marxism to Marxism-Leninism. According to Lenin, under capitalism the working class organizes itself in order to press its claims, not in order to start a revolution. It is the elite party that plays, and must play, the role of activist avant-garde, and its chances of success are dependent on the vulnerability of the capitalist system. And it is not in the most advanced industrial countries, but in the backward countries, that this vulnerability is greatest.

Trotsky had at first rejected the Leninist concept of democratic centralism, and Lenin had rejected the Trotskyist concept of a permanent revolution that in a barely industrialized country would gradually become a socialist revolution through an alliance of the workers and the peasants. The merger of these two ideas gave to Bolshevism its explosive force. We should add here that neither of the founders of Bolshevism felt he was betraying the Marxist heritage. Lenin never doubted for an instant that the party was not only the avant-garde but also the incarnation of the working class and its historic mission. Trotsky, for his part, regarded capitalism as one historic entity, which encompassed all capitalist countries; even if the revolution had snapped only "the weakest link in the chain," i.e., the least industrialized country, it was the system as a whole that had been struck.

Lenin and Trotsky believed themselves sincere Marxists even as they were scrapping essential portions of Marx's thought. They repudiated his vision of a parallelism between development of the forces of production and the succession of social systems; they forgot the famous formula which holds that "no social order ever disappears before all the productive forces for which there is room in it have been developed, and new, higher relations of production never appear before the material conditions of their existence have matured in the womb of the old society."[3] They implicitly dropped the primacy of economic forces in historical evolution.

The points of controversy among twentieth-century Marxists are apparent in this first phase. According to classical Marxism, the development of capitalism leads spontaneously to revolution. But if the standard of living of the masses rises instead of falling, if those entrusted with the historic mission are content with social reform and political democracy; in short, if economic progress thrwarts the catastrophes that would be the revolution's salvation, "What Is to Be Done?" On the other hand, Marxism is a theory of capitalism, but there are actually a number of capitalisms, and the Second International, according to the famous formula, was nothing more than a letter box. When capitalist countries make war upon one another, what is the duty of the workers, of Marxists, of the leaders of the International? *Prosperity* and *nations* are the two obstacles on which the unifying impulse of Marxist movements has regularly shattered.

At the beginning of the century, the Marxism of the Second International played only a minor part in the cultural life of Europe, including Russia. It would be difficult to name one economist, one sociologist, one historian of great stature, who explicitly called himself a Marxist. A Kautsky is not in the same class with a Max Weber, or even a Georg Simmel. Nevertheless, the Marxists of the pre-1914 German, Austrian, Italian, and Russian schools did participate in the development of the social sciences, did belong to the same universe as the non-Marxists, were "valid interlocutors" in the never-ending discussions on the destiny of modern societies. It would not be wrong to say, it seems to me, that the best of Marxism had been assimilated by Western culture. As for its political and prophetic ingredients, they were left to the "Marxists," i.e., to

[3] In the Preface to *A Contribution to the Critique of Political Economy* (1859).

doctrinaires and leaders of workers' movements. By 1914 these movements had ceased to frighten the bourgeois governments.

The revolution of 1917 opened a new era.

Victory and Decline: 1917–30

Prior to 1917, European and Russian Socialists had discussed in the abstract, so to speak, problems to which the events that began in 1914 gave a tragic urgency. There was no longer room for speculation, only action. One had to take sides—for or against the war, for or against the Bolshevik Revolution.

In 1914 the Second International ceased to exist. Every Socialist party, on its own and in its own way, had accepted the obligation of national defense, even if it had not subscribed to the Sacred Union. As for the ten days that shook the world in 1917 (i.e., the seizure of power by Lenin and company), they produced what one French historian has called the Great Schism: the final break between Socialists and Communists, between the Second International (more dead than alive) and the Third International, between reformers and revolutionaries.

Two questions dominated the debate. Was the Russian Revolution the one that Marx and the Marxists had anticipated and evoked with fervent wishes? Had the Messiah come or not? Whatever the verdict on Bolshevism, the Socialist parties outside Russia also had to decide whether they should submit unconditionally to the authority of the Third International, which meant, actually, to the Bolshevik party of the U.S.S.R.

In theory the non-Russian Socialists had three options. They could condemn the revolution of October 1917 out of hand and denounce the dictatorship of the party *over* the proletariat, which was falsely represented as a dictatorship *of* the proletariat. They could abstain from passing definite judgment on the revolution of 1917 but reject the statutes of the Third International and the subordination of the international working-class movement to a party merged with a national government—that of the U.S.S.R. Or, finally, they could submit to the

demands of the Third International, conceding that the socialist movement had indeed become inseparable from the
destiny of the Bolshevik Revolution, and that obedience to the
one Marxist party that had succeeded in coming to power was
both inevitable and justified.

In France and elsewhere a good many Socialists took the second position, at least verbally, during the period between the
founding of the Third International, or of a national Communist party, and the conclusion of the Nazi-Soviet pact of
1939. But the dialectic of competition inevitably led to hostility between the champions of the Second and Third Internationals, a hostility that was but thinly veiled at the time of
the Popular Fronts. The Communists denounced the "social
traitors," and, even as they cooperated with them, sought to in-
filtrate joint organizations with their own men, to take over key
positions, to win over the activists and voters of the party they
had pledged to work with. How could the Socialists have failed
to arraign in their turn the Communists and their methods?

Hopelessly at odds, Socialists and Communists alike were the
prisoners of a false consciousness, which Marxists had once been
pleased to unmask in their adversaries. The false consciousness
of the Social Democrats consisted of dressing up reformist practice in revolutionary ideology, in representing essentially national policies as international ones in speeches and congresses.
The false consciousness of the Communists consisted of painting over a line of action inspired by a revolutionary voluntarism with a doctrine positing objective laws of history, of hid-
ing an actual primacy of politics and party beneath a jargon
of "relations of production" and "class struggle." The false
consciousness of the Social Democrats has been commented
upon and criticized many times, recently by the Social Democrats themselves. It is not necessary for me to dwell upon it
further. The false consciousness of the Communists, on the
other hand, has been acknowledged and explained much less
frequently.

Marxist doctrine is one of both theory and practice, a dialectic between consciousness and action. It is in danger, therefore,

of leaning toward objective determinism, in which case it would favor adaptation (or resignation) to the inexorable laws of history. But it also is liable to lean in the other direction, toward voluntarism, and substituting party decree for the will of the masses or evolutionary trends. Bolshevism was a "voluntarist" reaction to the "determinist deviation" of the Second International, unless you prefer to call Bolshevism a voluntarist deviation, or heresy. One defines orthodoxy only by taking a position, since the sacred texts are ambiguous and since events have ruled out the centrist synthesis ("revolution through reform").

True, the war and its aftermath did foster revolutionary situations, but these derived neither from the development of the forces of production nor from the economic contradictions of capitalism. In the final analysis, events depended neither on the means of production nor on class relations, but on the party. In practice the Bolsheviks substituted the primacy of political action for the primacy of the forces of production. They concealed this revision by retaining the vocabulary of the class struggle, and by identifying the party with the class.

Once again Bolshevik Marxism made the most of ambiguities inherent in Marx's thinking. In his historical and sociological research, Marx had often recognized the relative freedom of action and effectiveness of political events, national states, wars, and armies—nothing prevented the Communists from acting in accordance with one doctrine and speaking in accordance with another without being aware of the contradiction. A technique for revolution and seizure of power, Bolshevism invoked the laws of history, which it freely adapted to the needs of its propaganda and to the course of events. The supreme triumph of voluntarism came with the first Five-Year Plan, when Stalin set goals at once unattainable and unquestionable, unleashing the terrible crisis of agrarian collectivization.

The disputes between Bolsheviks during this period (1917–30), although scarcely known in the West at the time, were as interesting as the debates that had accompanied the "Great Schism." Before 1930 the Bolsheviks argued among themselves over the organization of the state and the building of socialism. Westerners are realizing that factions inside the party were opposed to the totalitarian regimentation of all organizations, especially the trade unions. Other methods of industrialization, of "capital accumulation," were put forth. At the time people in the West were not sufficiently aware of the problems involved in choosing a technique of economic development to grasp the real scope of these controversies.

By contrast, the clash (more of myths than practices) between "socialism in one country" and "permanent revolution" caused a tremendous stir. The personalities of the leading contenders, the apparently world-wide significance of what was at stake, the renewed antinomy between the International and nations—all this helped to transfigure the interchange between Trotsky and Stalin, to lend it a tragic magnitude. In retrospect it is difficult to separate the polemics, an aspect of the struggle for power, from the purely theoretical discussion. Even if we assume that Trotsky and Stalin did hold differing views of the relations between the Soviet Union on the one hand and the Communist parties and the world revolutionary movement on the other, even if we suppose that in China or Germany Trotsky would have taken a different tack, circumstances allowed but limited room for maneuver. Since both saw the U.S.S.R. as the first socialist state and the center of world socialism, both would have had to work toward the development of socialism's temporary homeland while awaiting the opportunity to seize power elsewhere.

After 1917 the world-wide influence of Marxism changed in character. Marxian thought lost what Soviet reality (or illusion) gained. There was less talk of absolute or relative pauperization, of the law of gradual decline in the rate of profit—more about the meaning, the setbacks and successes, of the Russian Revolution. Neither the Marxists nor the non-Marxists as yet made any effort to interpret this revolution by the method used by Marx himself in *The Eighteenth Brumaire of Louis Bonaparte*.

Then, too, I have the feeling that on the intellectual plane the victory of 1917 contributed to the decline of Marxism. The survivors of the Second International prolonged their labors without renewing their ideas. No new Mondolfos or Labriolas appeared in Italy, no new Kautskys or Hilferdings in Germany, no Jaurès in France. Only the Austrian school, with the Kantian Marxism of Max Adler, still had a certain vitality. Classical Marxism had lost its power of attraction. Bolshevik activists and apologists were recruited among men of letters or scientists. Neither Paul Langevin, a great scientist, nor Louis Aragon, a great writer, had any effective knowledge of economics or sociology. The Social Democrats, rightist revisionists, were condemned to participate in the management of bourgeois society; Marxism, the pessimistic science of capitalism, was not of much help to them, teaching as it does the irreducibility of the contradictions that they, as managers of bourgeois society, had the immediate task of mitigating. The Communists, left revisionists or voluntarists, were led gradually into dogmatism. Masters of a supposedly socialist country, the Bolsheviks had to justify their actions in terms of the doctrine in whose name they had triumphed. But the doctrine was of little more help to them in the managing of their new state than it was to the Social Democrats in their management of the bourgeois state. The Social Democrats resorted to the expedient of projecting the reconciliation of events and predictions, of their practice and their theory, into the distant future. The Bolsheviks, however, had to proclaim, if not achieve, this reconciliation at every moment. By the time Stalin gained totalitarian power, around 1930, only the orthodox version of the doctrine was tolerated, and it was imposed on the Third International by one omnipotent man. And the facts themselves were doctored as necessary to make the orthodoxy true.

The Period of the Personality Cult

Debate ceased inside Russia in the early thirties, when the era of the Great Lie began. Until 1953 Stalin, and Stalin alone, decided what was the correct interpretation of Marxism and what the dogma would contain. The realm of "state truths" was enlarged to an inordinate extent, eventually including such day-to-day matters as the necessity of tractor stations, the percentage of national income to be set aside for investment (fixed at 25 per cent), and even scientific thought (one thinks of Lysenko, Michurin, the condemning of bourgeois genetics and Einstein's relativity). Stalin's pronouncements on linguistics and his final treatise on economics were immediately incorporated into the dogma, to become the subject of endless commentary by Communist "ideologues" in Russia and abroad.

Of all the Bolsheviks only Trotsky, his life in constant danger, pursued from his exile the debate against Number One, who had become master of both the party apparatus and the state. To the bitter end the organizer of the Red Army remained loyal to Lenin, and demanded that he himself be given his due for his role in the 1917 revolution. Until the end of his life he claimed that the Soviet Union was a proletarian state—despite the process of "bureaucratization" he himself had mercilessly denounced. From the study of the French Revolution, he borrowed the concept of the Thermidorian reaction, which he often used to describe Stalin's regime. In opposition to this, he demanded a return to free discussion inside the party, a freedom which had, in fact, existed under Lenin and for the first few years after his death, but which even in Lenin's day had been denied to Mensheviks and Socialist Revolutionaries. When in power Trotsky had not always been more inclined to "liberalism" and moderation than Stalin. Undoubtedly he would not have eliminated his rivals after spectacular trials in which the defendants, Lenin's comrades-in-arms, confessed to fictitious crimes before thoroughly disabused judges. The regime's style was set by the personality of Stalin, a personality at once intellectually mediocre but powerful and monstrous. But it was Trotsky himself who had had the premonition that Lenin's concept of "democratic centralism" would lead to the replacement by one man of the Central Committee, the party, and even the proletariat. This leader of the revolution had perhaps never been so great as in misfortune. Pursued across the world by a vengeful despot, his children dying mysteriously one after another, he never abdicated. He kept on hoping for other revolutions, which he expected to follow the Second World War; the Soviet Union, now the victim of bureaucratic degeneration, would be regenerated; instead of being confined to a single country, socialism would once again be an international movement. Trotsky wrote somewhere that if history took a different course, it would then perhaps be necessary to resign oneself to regarding the Marxist hope of social revolution as a myth belied by the supreme judge: History.

Trotsky's polemics have an element of pathetic greatness, but they remain on the fringe of that History which Marxists never tire of invoking. Soviet reality was not what the revolutionaries had imagined it would be before they seized power. No, indeed —but in the name of what could they call their dreams right and reality wrong? Forced industrialization? Trotsky himself had favored it. Stalin had appropriated, and in his own way carried out, the platform of the left opposition; so again, on what principle could one renege? Everyone found quotations from Marx to justify his proposals, but in fact Marx could not possibly have anticipated—much less solved—the problems of economic development in a predominantly agrarian country governed by a party in the name of a dictatorship of the proletariat. Within the Bolshevik cadre the Trotskyist opposition did not lack for arguments, but none was decisive. It would have been necessary to call into question Lenin, democratic centralism, "the weakest link in the chain," and finally the Revolution itself.

In any event, there was no way for Trotsky to alter his fate after 1930. There were only two possible positions left for a Marxist—the Social Democrats' or the Communists', the reformists' or the revolutionaries'. True, both were open to criticism. The Social Democrats could have been more effective reformers; the Stalinists could have been less cruel in building socialism. The critics of the social democracies could go on living in them, but the Stalinists' critics instantly became traitors or agents of the Gestapo. Trotsky, who had organized and commanded the Red Army, was nothing more than the theorist and leader of an international sect that was torn by doctrinal bickering echoing the quarrels of the pre-1917 Russian Socialists. But the repetition was tragicomic.

The party of Stalin remained a monolith for some twenty-five years, but it did not have the same "impact" on the West before and after the Second World War.

During the thirties the Great Depression lent a measure of actuality to the old Marxist theories about the inevitable catastrophe in which capitalism, doomed by History, would be swallowed up. But the one who came up with a theoretical interpretation of semipermanent unemployment, or insufficient aggregate demand, of excessive savings, was not a Marxist, and it does not appear that John Maynard Keynes ever read *Das Kapital* very carefully, or took the distinction between value and prices very seriously. Even so, in his *General Theory of Employment, Interest, and Money* he did allude to a current of thought to which he himself adhered, to the pessimist school that foresaw the decline or paralysis of capitalism. The American economists speculating on the "maturity" of capitalism (e.g., Alvin H. Hansen) were also, in this sense, Marx's heirs.

Now, while the Great Depression was leading some bourgeois economists to rediscover and renew Marxist ideas (Marxist in the broad sense of the term), scarcely any Marxist economists or sociologists were making original analyses of the historical situation. To profit from the progress that had been made in economic thinking since Ricardo and Marx, one would have had to dispense with the conceptual apparatus of *Das Kapital*. Bourgeois economists refreshed their knowledge, whereas Marxist economists were content to proclaim that Marx's predictions had come true, and that the bourgeois governments would be incapable of overcoming the contradictions inherent in capitalism or of curing its evils.

Instead of making the working-class revolution inevitable, the crisis of capitalism swelled the ranks of other revolutionary parties—national and anti-Marxist parties. This fact had a double significance. In 1914 the workers as well as their leaders had demonstrated that they had a country, a fatherland; the nonworker masses, struck by the Great Depression, repeated the demonstration. Only a minority of the working class was willing to follow a party that acknowledged its subservience to a foreign party that had been merged with a foreign government. The nonproletarian masses, for their part, rallied not to workers' parties but to parties that borrowed their techniques in the name of an authoritarian national ideal. That the Fascists and National Socialists had the backing of Big Money is beyond doubt. But to reduce the victories and regimes of Mussolini and Hitler to phases or forms of monopoly capitalism is to fall victim to a detective-story concept of history and to misconstrue obvious facts. A capitalist society, even one shaken by an unprecedented crisis, does not spontaneously polarize into two blocs, one bourgeois, the other proletarian. Both the middle and the working classes become divided. The moderate middle-class parties draw closer to the anti-Bolshevist working-class party. And the Bolsheviks find themselves in temporary alliance with the extremists of the right against formal or bourgeois democracy. Here again voluntarism prevails—in the sense that the decision by the men in Moscow of the line to be followed by the German Communist party determines events whose "laws" one would seek in vain.

A Marxian analysis, i.e., one that seeks to relate the attitudes of different social groups to socioeconomic circumstances, was by no means unsuited to the ups and downs of European politics between the two world wars, provided one took the same liberties with the method that Marx himself had taken in his historical writings. The connection between socioeconomic circumstances and political attitudes and positions is always discernible, but it is not strictly predetermined or at the very least not predictable. Prejudices, value systems, ideological convictions come between the crisis or proletarization process and the reactions of individuals and social strata. True, these reactions are influenced by what "monopolistic capitalism" does, but monopolistic capitalism cannot create out of nothing the emotions it exploits. After he has taken over the state, the charismatic leader makes decisions himself, and he does not necessarily obey those who have allowed him to come to power.

Despite the mediocrity of Marxist thought during the years of the personality cult, Communism—or, more precisely, the Soviet experience—exerted a profound influence on the political life and ideological controversies of the West. The cause of this apparent paradox is simple. Before 1939 most of those who rallied to the Soviet cause were ignorant of Stalinist reality, or refused to look at it. They were reacting to the crisis in the West, and seeking in the East an ideological fatherland because they were in revolt against their own society. Never was the Soviet regime more cruel than between 1930 and 1938, the years of agrarian collectivization and the Great Purge; never did it seduce more minds, even in the United States. After 1945 the Soviet Union was crowned with the halo of its army's victories, transfigured by its power in the eyes of worshipers of History. The very madness of the despot contributed to the bewitchment of the faithful and of fellow travelers. In regimenting the speech of millions of men—even of free men—Stalin became a kind of high priest, the Père Ubu of a sacred and bloody mystic rite.

Between the periods 1930–39, on the one hand, and 1945–55, on the other, there is one major difference. Prior to 1939 democrats regarded National Socialism as the immediate danger. The imperialism of the Third Reich gave rise to the Popular Front and Franco-Soviet rapprochement, and made probable a common struggle of the bourgeois democracies and the Soviet Union against "fascist" countries. After 1945, however, the fascist threat had ceased to exist, except in Communist propaganda, and the sovietization of eastern Europe spread fears that the Russian Empire and a Communist ideocracy would be extended to the Atlantic.

Too, the postwar years in Continental Europe, especially in France and Italy, were filled with the tumult of ideological debate. A rather strange debate, one might add. In theory we anti-Communist democrats should have been debating with the spokesmen for ideological orthodoxy. But how could one seriously debate with intellectuals, almost all of whom were shameless mediocrities, and all of whom were bound to a discipline that is always restricting, no matter how much the party line fluctuates? For want of a worthwhile interlocutor among the Communist true believers, we had to look around for some among the fellow travelers. These, for their part, tried to strike up a dialogue with the orthodox, or at least be recognized by them as allies. Depending on the circumstances, they were either cast into the outer darkness or tacitly tolerated. We laid before the Communists the facts verified by Khrushchev's speech to the Twentieth Party Congress, but any mention of them prior to 1953 was taken as a sign of prejudiced anti-Communism. With the subtle Marxism of Maurice Merleau-Ponty or Jean-Paul Sartre a philosophical dialogue was possible.

Dogmatic crystallization of Stalinized Bolshevik Marxism after 1930; mediocrity of Social Democratic thought, torn between an ever more theoretical adherence to the Marxism of Marx (in the centrist version of the Second International) and reformist policies that would have required an understanding of the capitalist system: this was the outcome of the Great Schism between Communists and Socialists, of the refusal of both to accept a course of history that did not fit the framework of their philosophy. Missing from this sketch is an element the political importance of which is almost negligible, but which rates mention in the history of ideas: Hegelianized Marxism, now leaning toward the Bolsheviks, now toward the Social Democrats, now locked in opposition to both—the last a curious position for a philosophy that claimed to be a union of theory and practice.

The Hegelian existentialist Marxist movement seems to me to have passed its peak and to be in decline, even in France. In the United States those who carry on the Marxist tradition fall into two groups, the second apparently the larger. The first group criticizes capitalism as an economic system, accusing it of exploiting the masses, or of not fully utilizing the forces of production, or of churning out useless merchandise, or of sacrificing millions of victims along the way—all this, and more besides, at the same time. The second group moves from socioeconomic criticism to cultural criticism, making its target either mass culture (the stupefying of the individual by culture industries) or the monstrous crimes committed in our era (wars, concentration camps, genocide), attributing these to capitalism by identifying a system defined by specific characteristics (private ownership of the means of production, market mechanism) with a concrete historical entity. If, having lost either their faith or their Mecca, many Marxists hold out against conservatism and denounce a false culture, it would be wrong to think that these disappointed, unrepentant Marxists have a monopoly on such criticism. They have simply joined the large army of those who do not expect a revolution, i.e., replacement of private ownership of the means of production with collective ownership, to miraculously change man's lot. Which does not mean that Marxists must now be resigned to the evils they have hitherto denounced. All they have to do, instead of dreaming of revolution, is think about reform.

The Legacy of De-Stalinization

Between 1945 and 1953 the Soviet Union and the entire Soviet bloc seemed so monolithic that observers ended by losing any sense of historical perspective. Fascinated by Stalinism, they wound up regarding this almost aberrant episode as the essence of the Communist movement. Within the Second International the Russian Social Democrats were notorious for their propensity to factional conflict and schism. Once launched upon revolutionary action and finally in power, the Bolsheviks quarreled every time a big decision (October *coup d'état*, peace of Brest-Litovsk) had to be made. Though Lenin, obsessed with the example of the French Revolution, had solemnly warned against crossing the "blood line," they wound up killing one another right and left, or, rather, were practically all slaughtered at the orders of the man they had chosen as General Secretary of the party. The struggle for power was intensified by the practice of turning the preferences and ambitions of each faction into ideology.

When the Stalinist façade collapsed after 1953, the Communists became their old selves once again; delivered from the fear inspired by a ubiquitous police force and a despot who was publicly adored and privately hated, they reverted to their true nature and resumed their historical-ideological debates—debates that were the more numerous and impassioned because several other countries were now laying claim to the same doctrine, and each of these countries, even if it was itself a monolith (which was not the case), spontaneously wished for some autonomy vis-à-vis Big Brother.

The official dogma, which was inordinately extended during the period of the personality cult, has shrunk to several simple propositions: public ownership of the means of production; identification of the party with the class; insistence upon an irreducible contradiction between class societies and socialist societies (defined by the power of the Bolshevik party); the inevitable decay of capitalism and final victory of socialism; rejection of ideological coexistence, i.e., of any questioning of theses that party leaders declare to be doctrinal truth at any given moment. The more limited this truth becomes, the more room there is for social, political, and economic debate within the Communist framework.

Some of this debate, however, cannot help touching the dogma itself, and shaking it. Here, it seems to me, are the main controversies which Khrushchevism gave rise to and which threaten the integrity of the dogma itself.

The Controversy About the Past. Once the personality cult has been acknowledeged, once the crimes of the Great Purge and the concentration camps have been confessed, how can one maintain party infallibility? How can one claim superiority for the Soviet system over all others? How is one to explain the cult itself? Western Marxists find it easier to answer these questions than orthodox Marxists. We shall always find an Isaac Deutscher to explain that the barbarism of the Russian people could be uprooted only by barbarous methods, a theorist of development to suggest that the Soviet concentration camps are the equivalent of child labor during the first decades of the last century in England. Peter Wiles will stage an ironic dialogue between the theoretician of historical determinism and the simple historian; the latter will have an answer for all the arguments of the former, and will suggest, without demonstrating it, that the horrors of agrarian collectivization and the Great Purge were unnecessary for development and would not have occurred if not for Stalin.

None of these interpretations is wholly acceptable to the Soviet Communists. That one man alone can be responsible for such events ill accords with the vision of a history governed by objective laws. That economic systems and plannng techniques depend upon the level of development is a thesis dangerously close to a view of history more appropriate to a Rostow than to a Communist. The Russians would not willingly subscribe either to the explanation that "barbarism has to be fought by barbarous methods," the obstacle here being, if not their Marxism, at least their national pride.

Hence there is no way for the Communists to return to their former dogmatism once they have admitted the facts of the personality cult. The despotism of one man *over* the party, or *with* it, has demonstrated that power in the hands of the party does not necessarily mean the liberation of the proletariat.

The Economic Controversy. Correctly or incorrectly, the Communists have derived certain economic ideas from *Das Kapital:* price should not be a function of scarcity but of the cost of production (to be calculated, if possible, in terms of hours of labor) ; the constant rate of interest should not play an active role, but at most should encourage businesses not to overstock; indicators intended for the heads of business enterprises should be objective, quantitative, expressed in units of value. If a profit indicator is introduced, the prices must be *real prices,* and not arbitrarily fixed by planning agencies. Personally, I do not think that such reforms are incompatible with *Das Kapital,* in which Marx did suggest what would amount to a noncapitalist economy, but never analyzed its methods in detail. The fact remains that the reforms advocated by the more daring Soviet economists tend toward re-establishment of some sort of market, hence toward a Soviet economy whose functioning is more like that of Western economies.

On Intellectual Freedom. During the period of the per-

sonality cult, party dogma was at once so broad and so imperative that agreement between the orders issued by the regime
and the words spoken by the intellectuals was spontaneous and
immediate. The latter did not pretend to fix their own margin
of freedom; once the party had spoken, they knew what they
had to say. Even in relation to painting, music, and sculpture,
the theory, if not the actual practice, was beyond doubt or
criticism. This is no longer true today. In his speech on culture
Khrushchev abjured setting up his own taste as a criterion of
beauty. But the boundaries between intellectual freedom and
the categorical condemnation of ideological coexistence are uncertain. At what point does social criticism, as expressed in a
novel or a comparison of the Soviet and Western systems, become the heresy of "ideological coexistence"? In a sense it is
more difficult to allow some intellectual freedom than to sup-
press it completely.

Relations Between Communist Countries. Marxism is weak
on the subject of international relations. The Leninist theory
of imperialism, a simplification of English ideas (in particular
J. A. Hobson's), has been incorporated in the Marxist canon.
Imperialism is viewed as the inevitable expression of monopoly
capitalism, just as the state is considered a mere instrument of
oppression in the hands of the ruling class. By deduction from
these axioms it follows that Communist countries are all brothers and that none of them can be imperialist because all conflicts between countries have economic causes and stakes, and
since these causes and stakes disappear with the disappearance
of capitalism, conflicts between Communist countries are inconceivable. In actual fact, relations between Communist countries involve the same risk of conflict as relations between non-
Communist countries. The frontier between Rumania and
Hungary, the fate of Transylvania, affects the two nations—
rulers and populations—regardless of their socioeconomic system. Communist China does not agree that Outer Mongolia
is part of the Soviet Union, and is perhaps not happy about
conceding it the Maritime Territory either.

On the economic plane, trade between Communist countries

has led to some disputes. The terms of trade for goods whose prices are arbitrarily set in each country are open to arbitrary manipulation. After 1956 Khrushchev admitted that Polish coal had been acquired at an artificially low price, and agreed to make supplemental payments to Poland. Even referring to the world price on the capitalist market is no guarantee of fairness.

Being allies and members of the same bloc leaves Communist countries many opportunities for disagreement with one another. The small ones may want to assert their independence of Big Brother; or they may have a different idea of what is in the bloc's interest; or the national interest of one bloc member may clash with what the Soviet Union considers the bloc's higher interests. Yugoslavia broke away to protect its control of domestic affairs, China because it did not want to be subordinate to the Soviet Union and because it considered Khrushchev's strategy contrary to its own interests and to the interests of Communism and Marxist-Leninist ideology.

Even so, relations between Communist countries are not exactly the same as relations between Western countries. Adherence to a common ideology helps both to unite and to divide them. United by the feeling of having common enemies, they are divided in the ideological formulation of their positions. They have not learned how to accommodate to their way of thinking and acting differences of opinion and antagonisms that are considered normal in countries not ruled by ideology.

War and Peace. This is the last and most serious controversy. If nuclear armaments have ruled out war as the last phase of the historic transition from capitalism to socialism, how can the feeling of a death struggle between the two blocs be sustained? And how can the hope of victory be kept alive in the Communist parties of the industrialized countries?

The issue of peaceful-coexistence versus final-victory-of-Communism repeats on an international level the reform-versus-revolution dialectic of the Second International. At the beginning of the century the question was whether reform would or would not lead to revolution. Bernstein and Lenin both were inclined to give a negative answer, though the practical conclusions they drew from this were diametrically opposed. Today the Chinese and the Russians are wondering, the former openly, the latter secretly, whether without a war peaceful coexistence will ever lead to the destruction of capitalism. The Chinese are no more lighthearted than the Russians about the prospect of atomic war. But they are less hesitant than the Russians to support wars of national liberation, and more hesitant than the Russians to rule out once and for all, in so many words, a decisive war between the two camps.

Communism and the Underdeveloped Countries. To the five currently acknowledged subjects of debate we should perhaps add a sixth: How can one account for the variety of systems flourishing in the Third World? On this point Communists would seem to have no choice but to return to 1917, i.e., to the day events obliged them to abandon the thesis that the development of the forces of production parallels the development of socialism. The classical Marxism of the Second International did not anticipate history's skipping, or jumping over, the capitalist phase, since socialism was supposed to be nurtured by capitalism, as capitalism had been by feudalism. Men ask only the questions they can answer. The vision of parallel growth of the forces of production and the development of social systems was replaced by Trotsky's image of the weakest link in the chain. If you take not one capitalist country but the whole capitalist world as your field, the explosion of revolution in a single barely industrialized country seems less of a blow to the doctrine. Even so, the spokesman for the new state felt it necessary to expound the paradoxical thesis that the fatherland of socialism still had to "catch up" with the United States, thus indirectly admitting that the most progressive system in the world was at the same time economically behind.

To the extent that the "building of socialism" progressed, the paradox tended to disappear. After the Second World War the Soviet Union became one of the two greatest military powers on earth, and if its per-capita output still lags behind that of western European countries, it is nonetheless second only to the United States in gross national product. Socialism is now identified with economic and military power, rather than a high standard of living.

Since the twenties, the Communists, encouraged by their own experience, have been staking their hopes on the "underdeveloped" countries of the Third World. Since they accepted Lenin's analysis of imperialism, they readily believed that revolt by colonial or exploited countries—particularly the two largest, India and China—against imperialist domination would be a fatal blow to the capitalist system.

In a sense their assessment of the revolutionary potential of Asia has been borne out by events, though, like good Marxists, the Soviet leaders were banking on the working class, not the peasant mass, to be the ultimate instrument, if not agent, of the so-called proletarian revolution. But Communist expectations have been radically belied on one very essential point: loss of their colonial empires has not weakened the capitalist mother countries in the least, and has not caused their standard of living to collapse. On the contrary, since 1945 growth rates in the West have been higher than they ever had been in the previous century or first half of this century. At the same time, no depression has occurred, and cyclical fluctuations, although they may still occur, have been less severe.

The creation or re-creation of some sixty countries in the short span of some twenty years, some by dint of their own efforts, others as a gift, raised two kinds of questions for orthodox Marxist-Leninists. First, how should these countries be classified? What categories did they fall into? How did they stand in relation to the two principal systems of our time, capitalism and socialism? Second, what method of development should they adopt? Did the Soviet Union have a concept of development to oppose to the Western concept (or the several Western concepts)?

To the first question the answer given during Stalin's reign was simple, even primitive: Either the independent countries would rally to the socialist camp and adopt a communistic government, or they would continue to be the victims (voluntary or involuntary) of capitalist exploitation. Stalin's Manichaeism

—capitalism or Communism, there is nothing in between—was matched, incidentally, by Dulles' unshakable stand, neutrality is immoral. When Stalin's successors decided to pursue a more flexible foreign policy and to exploit the rivalries and tensions among capitalist countries or between them and the newly independent countries to their own end, this crude black-and-white picture of the world was dropped. The "national bourgeoisie" was considered "progressive" to the extent that it tried to win or maintain national independence and to shake off the imperialist yoke. In the struggle against imperialism the masses, and above all the proletariat (i.e., the Communist party), were the most valiant fighters, but they could and should allow the struggle to be directed temporarily by the national bourgeoisie. But what happens the day after independence is won?

The Moscow theoreticians find it difficult to set up a typology because of the number of applicable criteria, even within the framework of their own system of thought. Seen from Moscow, an underdeveloped country can be classified according to: (a) its attitude toward the two blocs; (b) the class in power; (c) the status or position of the Communist party; (d) the technique of economic development it adopts, and its economic relations with the capitalist world.

The Soviet theoreticians are guided primarily by their distinction between capitalist and noncapitalist roads to development after independence, without reverting to a simplistic contrast between total socialism (Communist party in power) and total capitalism (Communist party not in power). A system midway between these two has now been identified as National Democracy, whose principal characteristic seems to be, official nonalignment notwithstanding, a diplomacy relatively favorable to the Communist camp, coupled with revolutionary rhetoric embodying themes or phrases taken from the Communists. As of now three countries, Guinea, Ghana, and Mali, have been christened National Democracies; a fourth, Indonesia, has been admitted to the category with some reservations. These countries, or at least the first three, have a single, but not Communist, party; espouse a relatively pro-Soviet neutralism; and play down the role of the market economy and private ownership.

Thanks to this concept of National Democracy, the Soviets have divided underdeveloped countries into three categories:

1. Independent countries ruled by the national bourgeoisie, in which capitalism is still the dominant influence.

2. National Democracies that have only one party, espouse pro-Soviet neutralism, and operate planned economies.

3. Communist countries.

Other writers have arrived at a more complicated classification composed of six types:[4]

1. Relatively advanced capitalist countries, whose leaders come from the national bourgeoisie (India, Burma, Ceylon, Syria, Lebanon, Tunisia, Brazil, Mexico).

2. Countries in which feudal forces continue to operate, capitalism is less developed, and the national bourgeoisie is weaker, but which have a neutralist policy and are struggling for their independence (Iraq, Morocco, Nigeria, Somalia, Sudan, Cambodia).

3. Countries in which power is held by a reactionary bourgeoisie, often in alliance with great feudal landowners (the Philippines, Turkey, Malaysia, Thailand, Pakistan, many Latin American countries).

4. Countries on a noncapitalist road to development (Ghana, Guinea, Mali, to some extent Indonesia).

5. Countries under imperialist domination (former French West Africa, Madagascar, Congo-Leopoldville).

6. Countries in a feudal state but having a neutralist policy (Nepal, Saudi Arabia, Ethiopia, Afghanistan, Yemen).

It is very likely that some countries will change categories, or may already have done so—owing to shifts in diplomacy or domestic conflicts. What interests us here is the efforts of Communist theorists to elaborate a typology that takes into account

4 I have taken this classification from an article by Robert F. Lamberg, in *Europa-Archiv 1963*, "Die marxistische-leninistische Theorie von den Entwicklungsländern: Wunschdenken und Verwirrung" (pp. 567–76).

four variables—diplomatic orientation, class relationships, political institutions, economic institutions—and the implied admission that many combinations of these variables are possible.

At the same time the Communist theorists are resuming the dialogue, such as it is, with Western theorists. On both sides it has been necessary to admit one undeniable fact: If socialism is what the Communists say it is, and the Soviet system is the model, there is no parallel between development of the forces of production (or stages of economic growth, to use Western terminology) and the transition from capitalism to socialism. On both sides it has been necessary to acknowledge a second indisputable fact: The political systems of the underdeveloped countries are numerous and diverse, and not all one-party systems are necessarily Communist. One regime that did join the socialist bloc (Cuba) was not established by a Communist party. A typology of the political systems of our time must be based on combinations of many variables.

The Soviet theoreticians are semiparalyzed in their typological endeavors by their obligation to keep rediscovering, no matter what, Marxist-Leninist patterns. They continue to identify the proletariat (often nonexistent) with the Communist party, to use the term "feudal aristocracy" in a sense so vague that it ends up covering any conservative class or group of large landowners. They assume that state capitalism or planning is "progressive," refusing to accept certain kinds of evidence, such as the fundamental difference between the single African parties, like those of Guinea and Ghana—whatever their terminology—and the Communist parties of the Soviet Union or Czechoslovakia. Nevertheless, communication has been re-established, and two ways of interpreting modern political systems are taking shape: one is that of the Communists, who maintain that the prime factor is the economic regime; the other is the one popularized by W. W. Rostow, who takes as his point of departure the phases of economic growth. Each of the two viewpoints takes into account the other's prime variable. I do not know whether the book *The Stages of Economic Growth* ought to be regarded as the *Non-Communist Manifesto* of the twentieth century, but I do know that the Communists look upon the currently fashionable Western theory of industrial society or theory of growth as a challenge to their own philosophy of history. The Marxists' disputes among themselves have culminated in disputes between Marxists and non-Marxists. Or should we say between Eastern Marxists and Western Marxists? For is not Rostow's *Non-Communist Manifesto* in a sense more Marxian, if not more Marxist, than its author suspects?

The confrontation between the Soviet and Western systems, between those who call themselves socialists and those who do not like to be called capitalists, has become one of the dominant themes of a historical sociology inspired simultaneously by Marx and Max Weber. A scientific confrontation and, at the same time, a political dialogue.

Indeed, each of these systems perceives and understands itself in the light of one possible version of Marxism, and makes the other part of its vision. If we assume that development of the forces of production is the key factor, then the Western countries are at the forefront of historical evolution. The Soviet countries must try to catch up with them, and the gap will be narrowed as the Soviet standard of living rises. On the other hand, the key determinant may be the regime—property ownership, regulation or planning, the class or party in power. By Marxist hypothesis, a system of proletarian rule and state planning constitutes "the avant-garde of humanity," to borrow Auguste Comte's formula. Of course, in the mater of per-capita output, this avant-garde will have to catch up with the country that is still a prisoner of capitalist exploitation. But at least wherever the capitalists and exploiters are eliminated, imperialism disappears as well, and the classes that remain will not be enemies.

Even if both these outlooks fit into a Marxist framework, they are not equivalent. In the last analysis, the Communist interpretation rejects the primacy of the forces of production, i.e., of the infrastructure or what is commonly known as the economy. Communism is *voluntarist* and *political*. Revolution depends on human action; seizure of power by the party inaugurates a new era. Not that the class struggle suddenly ceases with the victory of the Communist party, but at least it changes in character. True, an Eastern Marxist could adopt the Westerner's simple idea that in the twentieth century underdevelopment favors revolution. But he hesitates to do so, because then how could he at the same time claim that the proletariat (very small, sometimes nonexistent) is the revolutionary class par excellence? How can one define the party and socialism in terms of a class which does not exist, and which will be created only gradually with the building of socialism under the direction of a Communist party?

It is no less true that the Western Marxists' interpretation of the two types of system is equally unreconcilable with Marx's Marxism. A continuous development of the forces of production *without* paralysis of a system based on private ownership and competition obviously conflicts with one aspect of Marx's thought, the aspect the Marxists themselves have always considered fundamental. Even if we rule that the Soviet system is not socialist (because of insufficient development of the forces of production), the fact remains that there are different ways to accumulate the capital necessary for industrialization—it can be accomplished by entrepreneurs or by a party, by collectivizing agriculture and bleeding the peasants, or by allowing the peasants to own land and have a decent standard of living, etc. —and that the choice of method depends on a variety of circumstances, at times even on one man.

In other words, it is impossible fully to reconcile the Marxism of Marx with the course of twentieth-century history if we take authentic Marxism to include at least both a scheme of historical development and a method of analysis. As we have seen, in the absence of parallel development of the forces of production and succession of social systems, the Marxists, now pessimistic, now hopeful, waver between revolutionary voluntarism and resignation to the spontaneous course of historical evolution. ("Capitalism brings war as surely as storm clouds bring the storm." "Economic growth brings catastrophe—or abundance.") They subordinate the forces of production to the class struggle, or the class struggle to the forces of production; i.e., they accept in fact the primacy of political action, or the primacy of the forces of production; in one case they are technicians of revolution, in the other, reformists.

If in one sense neither the Western nor the Soviet spokesmen, neither Rostow nor Khrushchev, are strictly faithful disciples of Marx, in another sense they are both Marxists. When in 1955–57 I gave the two courses that have since been published under the titles *Dix-huit leçons sur la société industrielle* and *La Lutte de classes,* a number of ex-Stalinists, disillusioned by the Twentieth Party Congress and the events in Hungary, seized on the theory of industrial society as a position from which they could rebound. Sovietism and capitalism, enemy brothers, resemble each other more than either admits. In the mid-twentieth century the major opposing forces were not different kinds of advanced economies, but advanced economies and underdeveloped economies—a thesis partly true, partly erroneous. Two industrialized societies belong to the same historical era; industrialized and unindustrialized societies belong to different eras; but the French society of 1950, incomparably less developed than the American, was nevertheless part of the same civilization, whereas Soviet society during the personality cult, in the Stalinist era, belonged to another world. The theory of industrial society is in danger of being spoiled by a vulgarized brand of Marxism that is now becoming fashionable. Playing down the differences between systems, explaining away Stalinism as a necessity of industrialization, predicting an inevitable rapprochement of Soviet and Western systems and the industrialization of the entire planet—all this is grist to the mill of vulgarized Marxism, or economism. But the lesson of our century is something entirely different.

A new era in human history has begun, or is about to begin. It matters little what date we give this technical or scientific revolution. In truth it might be better not to use the concept of revolution, which, despite the meaning it has had since the great French Revolution, still reflects something of its cosmological origins. The scientific revolution is not a moment in a cycle; it will not return, in a later phase, to its point of departure. It indicates a *mutation of society,* and not, as some would have it, a *mutation of man.* The mastery that man is in the process of gaining over the forces of nature is so superior to that of past societies that we are entitled to look upon the epoch that began in the sixteenth century, and is coming to fruition today, as one long transition from historical societies to scientific societies. The nineteenth-century sociologists' perception of this prefigured the decisive awareness that dawned after the Second World War. But those who grasp the situation today are not prophesying, and know why they cannot do so.

Sociological insight at the beginning of the nineteenth century came in reaction to two major events: the French Revolution and the beginning of industrialization. Every sociologist tended to treat one of these events as essential, to stress its assets or liabilities, to extrapolate the remote future from one of the trends observed at the time, and to imagine its culmination in a positivist or socialist society. Even the probabilist thinkers like Herbert Spencer and Alexis de Tocqueville, who left it to the future to choose between systems—despotism or freedom, a free, commercial society or a controlled, authoritarian society—emphasized one variable and speculated on the outcome. We know, or ought to know, that the outcome is a beginning, the beginning of an unpredictable adventure. Society is not a *totality* ruled by one dominant variable. The so-called capitalist system is not adequately defined by its laws of property ownership, nor by the choice between market and planning. So-called capitalist societies are ruled neither by determinism nor by an objective dialectic whose movement is determined exclusively by economic contradiction. No society, no epoch, constitutes a unified entity that can be summarized in terms of one cause, one value. Sociological and historical pluralism is not a confession of ignorance, but a recognition of the true structure of the sociohistoric world.

The relationship between the art, science, politics, and economics of a society can be considered dialectical, but this relationship, while perceptible after the fact, can rarely be predicted in advance. The power over nature that science gives societies neither rules out nor rules in irreligion. It does not remove the "agony of choice" between modes of property ownership and regulation of the economy, any more than it puts an end to politics, i.e., to the authority of the few (inevitable and never fully justified), or to rivalries within and between states. The philosophies of history based upon an all-inclusive determinism are not indemonstrable. They are false. Whether or not one believes in man's metaphysical freedom, the fact is that historical man does appear to be free. In each of his specific activities he is subject to the obligations of that practical or intellectual world which he has chosen to enter. The scholar, as scholar, is not a slave of society, and he is free to seek the truth. The state of the forces of production is not, in itself, a sufficient cause of any specific political or even economic system. Conversely, given an economic system (laws of property ownership, system of control), we cannot deduce with any certainty either its political system or its human relationships—i.e., the degree of exploitation or oppression. Finally, any social order *inevitably* confers on one man or several an absolutely disproportionate power over the destinies of his or their fellows. One can always say that Hitler was an expression of German monopoly capitalism, but if Hitler had been killed in the First World War, would a different expression of this same capitalism have behaved in the same way? Would he, too, have committed genocide?

In reflecting upon his conditions, man is tempted to be, by turns, proud and afraid of such indetermination. The freedom of the artist or scientist is our pride; the freedom of the political man means subservience to the constraints of action. The indeterminateness of the system sets limits to rationalization and bureaucracy. It makes the rivalry between parties and ideas meaningful. It makes it impossible to mistake social rationalization for historical Reason. It leaves men collectively and individually responsible for their own destiny, but this responsibility, being every man's, is no man's. The role of mass leaders in our century—of Lenin, Hitler, Stalin, Churchill—elates the adventurer and terrifies the sage. Is it possible for one man, one man alone, to do great good or great evil in certain circumstances? And if tomorrow there be other heroes of the same stature, they will have thermonuclear bombs at their disposal.

The theory of the stages of economic growth, a kind of Western Marxism, does not always avoid the pitfalls of vulgarized Marxism. By what right does one consign all unindustrialized societies to the same category—the traditionalist societies of the Central African tribes, for example, along with China, the oldest empire in history? Do the stages of economic growth offer a much more satisfactory schema than the succession of social systems—when corresponding "stages" can be, and are, reached in one place by nineteenth-century methods, in another place by twentieth-century methods; in one by a system of free enterprise, in another by a system of state planning? Is it right to postulate or suggest that different systems become alike once they have reached the same stage of growth? As if relative opulence can mean only one way of life, as if comfort were sufficient to gratify all human aspirations and to end all ideological and class conflicts. Is not dollar diplomacy, too, which has given birth to takeoff-point diplomacy, based on the simple notion that underdevelopment breeds Communism, and hence economic aid is the answer to the threat of revolution?

If the West has not been impervious to the seductions of Marxism, the Third World is the scene of its greatest triumphs. In Italy and France a fraction of the working class and a number of intellectuals see the world through the distorting lenses of Marxism. Twenty-five years ago Daniel Villey wrote that it was Marx's genius to have guessed the feelings of the proletariat, and to have worked out in advance a spontaneous philosophy for it to adopt. Historical experience moves us to modify this formula. The working classes are not Marxist either in the advanced Anglo-Saxon or Scandinavian countries or in a number of underdeveloped countries in which factory workers enjoy a semiprivileged status in relation to the peasant masses. Even in the Latin countries, where slow development and political and religious traditions have favored it, Marxism seems to decline as the standard of living rises and the economy expands. By contrast, intellectuals in the Latin countries, and even more those in the countries of the Third World, have not lost their attachment to Marxism, and above all to Marxism-Leninism; because Marxism, supplemented by Lenin's theory of imperialism, enables them to understand both exploitation in the colonies and widespread prosperity in the industrialized mother countries, to establish a link between these two phenomena. The essence of capitalism is seen not in American or European prosperity, but in the mass misery of Algeria, India, and Brazil.

There is indeed a kind of moral affinity (*Wahlverwandtschaft*) between the passions of the Third World's intellectuals and Marxism-Leninism. The image projected by capitalism in countries colonized or dominated by big companies, or by white minorities established on conquered territory, does resemble in many respects Marx's general picture of capitalism. Moreover, Lenin's idea that capitalism *necessarily* leads to imperialism, or could not exist without foreign markets and excess profits from colonies—and on this point he reverses Hobson's thesis, to which he owes so much in other respects—is readily accepted by intellectuals whose own homeland is poor and weak. Thereafter they can attribute their poverty and weakness to their old masters, who have waxed rich and strong at the expense of those they oppressed and exploited. From this point of view the misery of the Third World is a direct result of the West's prosperity, for which it was first the indispensable prerequisite.

In this simplified form, the theory is false. Capitalism can grow in intensity. The mother countries which have lost their empires continue to grow richer. Right-wing decolonizers have learned the cost of domination, and prefer to keep their investment capital at home. To prove that the industrialized countries of the Northern Hemisphere are today exploiting the underdeveloped countries of the Southern Hemisphere, one must now resort to subtler arguments: the terms of trade, for example, or the disparity between the prices of raw materials and the prices of finished industrial products. But it is still true that, in the past, colonial exploitation could have contributed to European industrialization, and probably did in certain cases, and that when they withdrew, the colonizers more often than not left the territories they had ruled over in an underdeveloped state.

But with the introduction of a third participant in the Marxist dialogue between East and West we have come to the fifth and final period, that of the second Great Schism, not between the Second and Third International, not between Social Democrats and Bolsheviks, but between Russians and Chinese —or should we say between the Third and Fifth International, between the new revolutionaries and the new revisionists.

The Present Phase

The debate between the Seventh Floor of the State Department and the Kremlin is semiclandestine, semipublic. Which of the two systems, the Soviet or the Western, will grow more like its rival? Which interpretation of history will ultimately be borne out by history? The interpretation that sees Communism as a harsh method of industrialization useful in underdeveloped countries? Or the one that heralds the extension of Soviet socialism to the entire world, even though it first appeared in an unindustrialized country? Will Communism grow bourgeois, and state planning more flexible? Will both systems be transformed simultaneously, each one influencing the other by its very existence? Will the dialectic of hostility and imitation continue until the two systems finally become identical, or will there be no ultimate resolution, merely unending interaction?

The Chinese are disrupting this dialogue even as it is becoming more amicable. Though the polemics between Moscow and Peking, like all polemics between Bolsheviks, follow specific rules that make them difficult to interpret, one can guess some of the new issues at stake in the debate between Marxist-Leninists (and not, as in the earlier stages, between Marxists). The first is the Chinese accusation that the Soviet Union was becoming bourgeois. Khrushchev freely admitted that good goulash is no detriment to socialism, and that a pair of substantial leather shoes is much more desirable than wooden ones. Such goals are surely not unbefitting a Marxist. When all is said and done, Marxism was betting on the abundance that capitalist development of the forces of production would make possible. In an oft-quoted passage in *The German Ideology* Marx himself says that if there is still poverty in the days following the revolution, "the same vile business will start up again." The accumulation of capital cannot be, in itself, the end of socialism; it is but a means.

When capitalist regimes are in power, prosperity is a threat to Marxism because it is likely to snuff out the revolutionary ardor of the masses; in a subtler sense, it is also a threat to Communist regimes in power. First, different Communist countries are at very different stages of development. Should not the more advanced countries come to the aid of the less favored? Is it right for some to harvest the fruit of their labors while others are still in the throes of early capital accumulation? What obligations accompany the brotherhood that Communist parties never cease proclaiming?

More serious still, the unequal development and hence unequal living standards of the Communist countries irresistibly suggest an interpretation of history that is more in keeping with Western Marxism than with Eastern, more with Rostow's than with the Kremlin's. If a country's living conditions depend not on the system but on the value of per-capita output, a competition in growth rates replaces the implacable struggle between systems. Whoever wins the competition, victory can only be very relative. The victor is merely *going faster* than the vanquished; there has been no contest between good and evil.

And that is not all. For the "building of socialism" to mean something more than a mere increase in production it has to retain some human or moral significance. Authentic socialism requires socialist men. Neither Marx nor Lenin ever said what the New, or Socialist, Man would be like. It is certain, though, that this man was not to resemble the man found in a bourgeois society. Now, there is nothing to indicate that Soviet youth, enjoying social priveleges, are any less eager than Western youth for the goods industrial civilization has to offer: comfort, cars, dachas. Not that there are not Komsomols ready to make sacrifices for a noble cause; there are. But the United States also finds volunteers for the Peace Corps by the thousand.

The disabused observer will reply that revolutionary faith does not stand up well under the wear and tear of time, that the utter impersonality of human relations at work and in everyday life needs to be offset by the intimacy of the family circle and leads to a kind of individualism or family-centered selfishness. Perhaps that is the destiny of modern societies. But this transformation, however inevitable, does lend weight to the charge of "embourgeoisement" brought by the brother parties, who are still very close to their revolution, very fervent, and very puritanical—puritanical because of their fervor, and also, perhaps, because of their poverty. They cannot conceive of socialism outside the discipline of collective organization, and they look with suspicion upon the first signs of relative prosperity in the Soviet Union, a prosperity that is qualitatively less different from the West's than ideologues may have wished.

Did Khrushchev deserve to be called a revisionist, a term first applied to Bernstein and since then always used by Marxists in a pejorative sense? The situation in 1965 is so different from that of 1900, one might simply dismiss the question. Bernstein observed that capitalism was not conforming to Marxist predictions, and from this drew certain inferences. Concerning socialism there are no Marxist predictions that events might disprove, and therefore one cannot accuse Khrushchev of noting such contradictions and drawing conclusions from them. Still, it is not impossible to see an analogy between the denunciation of Bernsteinian revisionism by orthodox Marxists at the beginning of the century and the denunciation of Khrushchevian revisionism by the Chinese more than half a century later.

First of all, one Marxist is always the revisionist of another

Marxist. An ideological movement inevitably involves a right and a left; the left thinks it alone is faithful to the inspiration of the prophet and accuses the right of betrayal. In Kautsky's eyes, Bernstein was a revisionist. Kautsky in turn became a revisionist, and even a renegade, when he refused to see the October Revolution as the first step on the road to the millennium. In Trotsky's eyes, Stalin himself, the proponent of "socialism in one country," was a "Thermidorian," i.e., a traitor to the revolution. How could Khrushchev, if he took his two theses of peaceful coexistence and buttered bread seriously, seem like anything but a revisionist to the dour, pure Chinese?

The analogy, it seems to me, goes further still. Khrushchev discovered the impossibility of keeping alive revolutionary tension in a stabilizing Communist regime, just as Bernstein recognized the impossibility of keeping alive revolutionary tension in a so-called proletarian party under a progressive capitalist regime. The Chinese were able to accept certain elements of de-Stalinization the more easily because they resorted to subtler governing procedures and did not have the equivalent of concentration camps and the Great Purge. But de-Stalinization has gradually brought with it seeds of liberalism and the (still timid) adaptation of certain Western techniques of managing an economy.

Here again, one cannot say that the Chinese are orthodox and the Russians revisionists. Marx had the temperament of a rebel, and unless he himself held power, it is hard to imagine him subjecting his thought and pen to the orders of any state, even a state that called itself Marxist. He wanted to go beyond formal freedoms, while preserving them. Khrushchevian liberalism, however, was still very relative. The right, or rather duty, of the party to direct intellectual and artistic life, to make writers and artists bow to the exigencies of politics, was not called into question. Ideological coexistence was rigorously condemned, which means that Communist ideology was true, endowed with Universal Truth, and that so-called bourgeois ideologies were radically wrong. In spite of everything, Khrushchev's Russia was opening its doors to Western influences, and, compared to Stalin's Russia, might have seemed liberal. Far from permeating everyday life and shaping men's minds, the doctrine, still the official state truth, degenerated into an "ideology" (in the derogatory sense in which Marx used the term). A conscious or unconscious justification for reality, Marxism was less the basis for an ideocracy than the camouflage for a satisfied bureaucracy.

And this bureaucracy, concerned for rationality, moved further and further away from the primitive methods used in earlier stages of planning. After making progress between 1953 and 1958, agriculture brought new disappointments each year to the leaders in the Kremlin. Cultivation of the virgin lands of Central Asia proved a costly error. Despite all the reforms, centralized authoritarian planning was running into ever greater difficulties. All the European Communist countries, not only the Soviet Union, are openly debating the reforms necessitated by the increasing complexity of an advanced economy. Now, these reforms can be labeled "revisionist" if we are agreed that a system is socialist only to the extent that planning is centralized and authoritarian. Indeed, most of the reforms being contemplated do entail borrowings from the market economy, or from the spirit of such an economy: restoration of a margin of free decision to the heads of enterprises; abandonment of arbitrary price-fixing by the authorities, with consideration to be given the relative scarcity of a product; more widespread use of interest; possible replacement of quantitative indicators with a profit indicator, as the more daring reformers have suggested. All these measures, whether adopted or under discussion, are steps toward rationalization in the eyes of the economists; to the ideologues, they may seem, and should seem, tainted with revisionism.

I have no doubt that the Chinese will be disposed to take every bit as much liberty with dogma as the Russians are now doing should the need arise. The fact is that because of the difference in the levels of development of the Communist economies (if one may be allowed to apply to the Communist world the law that Lenin formulated for the capitalist world), the

Russians and Chinese are pursuing different policies. But, unable to refrain from putting in ideological terms practices that arise more from circumstance than from doctrine, they accuse each other of deviation. Having criticized the Communes and the Great Leap Forward, the Russians inevitably appear as opportunists to the Chinese. The latter, by the implacable logic of dialectics, are dogmatists in the eyes of the Russians.

I do not claim, of course, that ideological debates are *the cause* of the split between Peking and Moscow. Perhaps it is a classical conflict between the interests of two great powers. Perhaps the Soviet Union, like Holy Mother Russia, fears the Chinese masses, "miserable and innumerable." Perhaps the territorial ambitions of Communist China have disturbed the men in Moscow. Or maybe the experience, in 1958, of the Chinese military operations in the Formosa Strait have made the Russians fear that the brother party will drag them into conflict with the United States. The preceding pages do not attempt any historical explanation of the Sino-Soviet quarrel. In keeping with the aim of this study, they attempt to interpret debates between Marxists, debates which give expression to the dialectic of a historical doctrine at grips with history itself.

We have not yet mentioned what the leading contenders consider the essential issue: world revolution. Did Khrushchev take no interest in the spread of socialism, as the Chinese claim? Was he more interested in an accommodation with the imperialists (i.e., with the United States of America) than in supporting wars of national liberation (which in Western language means attempts by Communist parties to come to power by force)? The Russians have replied that the Chinese are ready to set fire to the world, to unleash a thermonuclear war in which hundreds of millions of men would perish, whereas they themselves refuse to sacrifice the living to the dream of a socialist civilization to rise upon the ruins of an atom-smashed universe. We have no ground for imputing any intention of war to Mao Tse-tung. Peking's diplomacy, moreover, has never been imprudent, and several years ago the official truth in Moscow was that a nuclear war would bury capitalism, not civilization.

The Sino-Soviet quarrel really repeats within the Communist world the Second International's experience in the capitalist world. Whether in opposition or in power, the workers, the Communists, the proletarian parties, all have a homeland, a country. The Communists are no exception. By dint of his omnipotence, Stalin succeeded for several years in maintaining the appearance of a monolithic Soviet bloc (although he could not prevent the defection of Yugoslavia). China was too big and too proud to take Moscow's word as law. Stalin's successors did not have sufficient prestige to impose their will without recourse to force. De-Stalinization dealt a death blow to the myth of party infallibility (especially Bolshevik infallibility). In Europe, Rumania is refusing to abide by Comecon's directives; Albania is siding with Peking—mainly, it would seem, to keep Moscow at arm's length. The parties are "brothers," but each one wants to have as much autonomy as possible. Everything suggests that Communism cannot avoid becoming national even though Communists may continue to invoke the universal truth of Marxism-Leninism.

Whether it be a matter of defining common policy toward the imperialist enemy or of reconciling the different economic interests of the different members of the bloc, the Communist countries do not get much help from the doctrine that theoretically unites them. And perhaps the invocation of an ideology makes common action even more difficult. That the Chinese are prepared to take greater risks than the Russians in supporting wars of national liberation may be true. In the absence of ideology divergent strategic assessments would not generate so much passion. That the Russians wanted to preserve their monopoly on atomic weapons in the Communist camp, as the Americans did in the Western camp, is perfectly understandable. But countries calling themselves brothers cannot confess their selfishness; they must hide it under ideological formulas. Agreeing to disagree is easier for countries that are not bound by a common ideology.

What will be the impact of this polymorphic, polycentric Communism on the outside world? (I am assuming that Khrushchev's successors, even if they avoid a total break with

Communist China, will not restore the unity of the Communist world.) I would hesitate to make categorical judgments on this point.

In the prosperous West, the Communist parties, especially the Italian party, which is less sclerotic than the French party, will benefit from the autonomy fostered by the decline of Moscow's authority. Instead of being a kind of closed countersociety within Western society, the Communist parties will probably try to become revolutionary once again, by playing the reform game. The French party, crystallized in its conservatism as though it had been in power for forty years, *may,* under pressure and constraint, break out of the Stalinist prison it has locked itself into. The Italian party may follow the Nenni Socialists' example. "Popular Front" may be the next watchword. The European Communists have everything to gain from super-Khrushchevism, from increasing "nationalization" of their parties, in the service of a theoretically universal truth.

Of course, the same distintegration of the Communist bloc that on the political level gives the Communist parties a chance in the West is a blow to the power of the Soviet camp. The ideology will probably seem less convincing, less compelling, when it has multiple versions. But this assumption has yet to be proved. Religions did not cease to spread once they broke up into rival churches. Castro was not a Communist when he seized power, and today his relation to Moscow and Peking is more that of head of an autocephalous church than faithful worshiper at either of their churches. Other autocephalous regimes may appear in the Third World tomorrow. From now on, we shall have Communism without obedience to Moscow. The diplomatic scene will grow more and more complicated, and diplomats will pine for the good old days when the confrontation of just two blocs made it easy to distinguish between friends and enemies.

This story, like all true stories, is unfinished. It has no ending, no conclusion, but this does not proscribe all forward and backward glances.

It would be quite pointless to ask ourselves whether Marx,

who near the end of his life was already saying that he was not
a Marxist, would or would not be a Marxist-Leninist today. We
shall never know. A thinker, especially one like Marx, a philosopher of history, is bound too tightly to the problems, ideas,
and values of his own time to be transferable to a different
epoch, even as a game, without loss of his essential being, of that
which made him what he was. Having rebelled against the
cruelties of capital accumulation at the beginning of the nineteenth century, would Marx have turned his rebellion against
the bureaucrats of the Kremlin or the magnates of American
corporations a century later? Would he have looked around in
the Third World, like so many of his disciples, for opportunities to reanimate his indignation? In any case, he would have
found it difficult to accomplish now his feat of one hundred
years ago: today capitalism acclaims those who condemn it. His
books would be translated into all languages, and would be best
sellers or cause a scandal—which amounts to the same thing—
and would commend him to the attention of the Swedish
Academy.

Nor is it possible to assess Marx's share of the responsibility
for the way Marxism has turned out. No one will ever know
what the Russian Revolution would have been like in the absence of Marx's ideas. A revolution of some kind had become
probable, at least when bourgeois Europe started to destroy itself in a war to the death. But would it have followed the same
course if its leaders had not believed that they were the proletariat incarnate, that they were the avant-garde of world socialism? Or are we to assume that the revolutionaries would
somehow or other have found or thought up a doctrine to justify their actions? Logically, all things considered, Marxism
should have deflected the Bolsheviks from the road that they
took in 1917. As it was interpreted before 1917, Marxism suggested that it would be impossible to establish socialism in a
country like Russia, which had not yet passed through the stage
of capitalist industrialization. In this sense one can say that the
Bolsheviks took power and built their allegedly socialist system
in spite of their doctrine. Other Marxists, the Mensheviks, had

warned that an attempt to establish socialism in a country in which most of the population worked in agriculture would result in fifty years of despotism. Events proved them right, but did not save them from defeat and exile. True, most of the Bolshevik leaders themselves became the victims of their victory, and rather quickly.

The Mensheviks were not the only ones whose perception was unavailing. In our century Marxists have frequently fought and won, but they have rarely accomplished what they set out to do. Rarely have men who claimed to act in accordance with a science of history been so surprised by the consequences of their deeds—consequences foretold with great precision by other Marxists. Trotsky had foreseen where democratic centralism would lead. From time to time Lenin, but most often the Mensheviks, foresaw the consequences of an attempt to establish socialism in a predominantly agrarian country. Bukharin had foreseen the consequences of forced industrialization at the expense of collectivized peasants. But what they all failed to foresee was the capacity for progress and self-renewal of the system they have persisted in calling capitalism. Nor did they foresee the demoniac power of a minority determined to stop at nothing. Democratic socialism was built by workers' parties that had been converted from Marxism to pragmatism, whereas no socialist regime built by Communists has yet emerged from totalitarianism.

The lesson should be clear to all who prefer men to ideas, dialogue to violence. But experience proves that it is not. One reason for this is underdevelopment. In countries that lack an entrepreneurial class and an effective government apparatus, thanks to the resistance of the privileged classes, the Bolshevik technique, the mobilization of an entire people by one party in the name of an ideology, seems the only way. But this practical reason is not the only one. Though on the historical plane it is the most important, on the plane of ideas it is secondary. Marxism à la Rostow has no trouble taking into account the Communism of the underdeveloped countries. What is interesting is the obstinacy with which superior minds in the West retain their faith in Marxism. I am thinking of Jean-Paul Sartre, whose case is not unique. Others, too, like Herbert Marcuse, are apparently beyond cure of the Marxism contracted in their youth. True, it will be objected that Sartre himself has no great love for what Marxism has become.

Marxism has come to a standstill. Precisely because this philosophy wants to change the world . . . because it is and is intended to be *practical,* a real schism has occurred within it, with the result that theory is rejected on the one hand, action on the other. . . . The result of the separation of theory and practice was the transformation of the latter into empiricism without principle, the former into pure, congealed knowing. . . . Marxism, as a philosophical interpretation of man and history, necessarily had to reflect an unquestioning commitment to planning; this fixed image of idealism and violence did idealistic violence to the facts. For years the Marxist intellectual believed that he was serving his party by distorting experience, by overlooking embarrassing details, by grossly oversimplifying data, and above all by conceptualizing an event before he had studied it.[5]

Since 1917 the Communists have contributed nothing, or next to nothing, to the humanities and social sciences. Some Marxists, who have at times submitted to orthodoxy and at times broken out of their confinement, have made a modest contribution.

Sartre immediately adds, of course, that Marxism is, nevertheless, the unsurpassable truth of our time. "Marxism's arteriosclerosis is not the result of normal aging. It is caused by a peculiar world situation. Far from being worn out, Marxism is still very young, almost a child. It has barely started to develop. It is therefore still the philosophy of our time. It is unsurpassable, because we have not yet passed beyond the circumstances that created it. Our thoughts, whatever they are, can take shape only upon this humus. They must be contained within the framework it provides, or be lost in a vacuum, or retrogress."[6] I shall not discuss the basically Hegelian idea that

[5] *Critique de la raison dialectique,* pp. 25-26.
[6] *Ibid.,* p. 29.

one philosophy, and only one, dominates an epoch because it both summarizes its wisdom and expresses its being and will. Applied to Marxism in our time, this is really absurd. To agree with Garaudy, as Sartre does, that "Marxism today is the only system of coordinates that enables one to place and define a thought in any realm whatever, from economics to physics, from history to morals," is simple delirium, whether conscious or not. Neither Marx's Marxism nor the Marxism of the Communists in Moscow or Peking makes it possible to synthesize a universe of knowledge by now grown so rich that it defies any hope of synthesis. Encyclopedic minds no longer exist and, regardless of the school they belong to, philosophers cannot possibly encompass the whole of contemporary culture.

What Sartre's formulas come down to is that he thinks of Marxism as a *philosophy*, not as a *science*, even though it was Marx's purpose to elaborate a *scientific* analysis of capitalism. What Marx meant by science is certainly debatable. Let us grant that the term has kept something of its Hegelian meaning. The Marxist science of capitalism does not claim to be an operational science. It claims to be total yet objective, critical yet analytical. Marx gave his *Das Kapital* the subtitle *Kritik der politischen Ökonomie* because he believed that in going back from price to value he was grasping essential phenomena and the inner law of the system, and at the same time exposing what he considered the crippling illusions of bourgeois economists.

Sartre has given up referring to Marxism as a science, the more so because of the horror in which he holds the scientism of Engels and his disciples. He has christened it a philosophy. But, having brushed aside what serves as philosophy for the Marxists, i.e., the—to say the least—rough speculations of the *Anti-Dühring*, the unsurpassable philosophy of Marxism he is left with is nothing but vague general propositions such as, "The essential discovery of Marxism is that labor, as a historical reality and as the utilization of specific tools in a predetermined social and material environment, is the real foundation

of organized social relations."[7] Or, "Men make their history themselves, but in a given environment, which conditions
them."[8] Or, "The material mode of production generally dominates the development of social, political, and intellectual
life."[9] Such propositions, each of which calls for extensive comment, hardly amount to an unsurpassable philosophy. Where,
then, in the final analysis, is this unsurpassable philosophy, if
we eliminate both the speculation of the *Anti-Dühring* and the
vague primacy of labor and economic relations? There is a
third kind of text that may reveal the secret. "Any formal remarks," writes Sartre, "cannot, of course, begin to add *anything
at all* to the clarity of the synthetic reconstruction of Marx's
Das Kapital. They cannot even begin to be a marginal commentary on it. Indeed, by its clarity that reconstruction rejects
all commentary."[10] Now, at last, we have it. The unsurpassable
Marxism is, on the one hand, the anthropology of man, who
creates himself in the course of time through labor and the
class struggle; on the other hand, it is a synthetic reconstruction
of capitalism, i.e., a total interpretation of modern society, con-
taining a critique of what is and an announcement of what will
be. A synthetic and at the same time critical science of the present, inspired by atheism and a will to universality: this is the
"unsurpassable Marxism" of which Sartre could make existentialism the foundation. What Western Marxists have been unwilling to forgo is, precisely, a philosophy of history that would
present itself as a science and that would make what should be
and what will be emerge from what is.

The synthetic reconstruction of capitalism attempted by
Marx with the conceptual instruments available to him is hopelessly outdated. His historical scheme no longer works, unless
we add so many qualifying assumptions that it loses all meaning. In short, the economic and sociological theory of capitalism, which from his thirtieth year he regarded as the essence of
his work, has not escaped the common fate of all learned works.

7 *Ibid.*, p. 225.
8 *Ibid.*, p. 60.
9 *Ibid.*, p. 31.
10 *Ibid.*, p. 376.

It is still a monument, but it has been surpassed, because knowledge progresses and history continues. Hence those who, in spite of everything, still call themselves Marxists, without identifying Marxism with the catechism of Moscow, Peking, Belgrade, or Havana, can only choose between equally precarious solutions. One group travels in the opposite direction over the road that led Marx from the Hegelian left to economics and returns to his early writings, discovering in them an unsurpassable philosophy, though Marx thought he had surpassed it by 1848. The others cling passively to the letter of *Das Kapital*, and in doing so are comparable to biologists who would explain evolution exactly as Darwin did, paying no attention to genetics and mutations, or physicists who would reject relativity, quantum theory, or microphysics.

Indeed Marxism, which seems sclerotic and unsurpassable to Sartre, seems to me both surpassed and alive. Perhaps we are not capable of writing *Das Kapital* in the twentieth century because we have lost the ambition for a synthetic and critical reconstruction of modern society—or the illusion that such reconstruction is possible. But on the fringe of state orthodoxies and vain ratiocinations we have not given up trying to understand man's condition in history and the meaning of modern societies. After 1848 Marx believed that the true way to philosophize was to know the social world in order to change it. Strange Marxists, those who discourse upon alienation or try to change the world without knowing it.

Sartre's Marxism*

In *La Critique de la raison dialectique,* Sartre constantly asserts the truth of Marxism and says there is no going beyond it, at least in our time.

There was the period of Descartes and Locke, then the period of Kant and Hegel, and since then there has been the period of Marx. Each of the three philosophies has been in turn the soil

* *Author's Note.* In a letter addressed to Pierre Brissen I explained the circumstances under which I wrote this article, which originally appeared in the *Figaro Littéraire* from October 24 to November 4, 1964, at the time when my former classmate from the Ecole Normale Superieure received and refused the Nobel Prize for Literature: "The author of *La Nausée, Huis Clos, L'Etre et le néant* and *Les Mots* is undoubtedly a man of outstanding ability. Only the ignorant were unaware of this before the awarding of the Nobel Prize. Sartre may have remained unknown up to the time of the publication of *La Nausée,* but he was never unappreciated. A number of us, at the Ecole Normale, sensed his genius. But I am no fonder than the unwilling prize winner himself of the kind of academic eulogies that have been showered on him recently; they are particularly pointless in his case since they are addressed to a committed writer and yet deliberately disregard the causes which his commitment is intended to serve.

"I feel that it would not be fitting for me to make this an occasion for recalling memories of our youth together. Our friendship came to an end more than fifteen years ago, and although we now shake each other by the hand instead of proffering mutual abuse, we continue to live in different worlds. While enjoying those formal liberties that are more or less respected by the bourgeois democracies, Sartre reserves his sympathies for revolutionary regimes which, in his opinion, have the advantage of preparing the advent of true freedom. I think quite differently, but a settling of political accounts would be just as out of place today as a show of reconciliation or a harking back to the distant past.

"I should have much preferred to leave to others the task of commenting on Sartre's output, the richness and complexity of which cannot be dealt with in a hastily written journalistic article. I have finally yielded to editorial insistence, but I shall have to be excused for limiting myself to remarks on *Critique de la raison dialectique,* which I reread last summer. I make no claim to having exhausted the subject announced in the title. It is easy to show that Sartre, in spite from which all individual ideas sprang and has formed the cultural horizon. In each case, the philosophy has proved impossible to surpass during the continuance of the historical period of which it was the expression.[1]

Similar statements, equally solemn in tone, occur frequently throughout the book: "I have said, and I repeat, that dialectical materialism is the only valid interpretation of the history of mankind. . . ."[2]

If we ask what doctrine is referred to in these declarations of allegiance, we find that the essential discovery of Marxism is that labor is the true foundation on which social relationships are organized. Since the concept of the true foundation is no less ambiguous than that underlying the expression "in the last analysis," dear to Engels, I personally am quite prepared to accept this essential discovery without, at the same time, aspiring to the honor of being a Marxist.

The vague and abstract statements of which the Marxism supported by Sartre seems to consist are made still less impressive by the fact that the entire aim of the section entitled: "The Question of Method" is to defend the *irreducibility* of the various spheres of human existence against bad Marxists. Referring to the thought of the Marquis de Sade, Sartre writes that "an ideological system is an irreducible entity"[3] and that the idea must be studied in all its developments. Nor does he hesitate "to recognize the originality of the sociopolitical groups thus formed and to define them in their very complexity, in spite of their incomplete development and their distorted objectification."[4] Similarly, existentialism can only assert the specific na-

---

of his efforts, does not manage to turn himself into a good Marxist, but why does he attach so much importance to being one? To adopt his vocabulary, his way of being a Marxist is by Being-what-one-is-not or Not-being-what-one-is. In more ordinary language, he is acting in good faith when he convinces himself of his belief in a form of Marxism which is rejected by the Marxist-Leninists and would probably have surprised Marx himself."

1 *Critique de la raison dialectique*, p. 27.
2 *Ibid.*, p. 134.
3 *Ibid.*, p. 76.
4 *Ibid.*, p. 81.

ture of the historical event; it endeavors to restore to that event its function and its multiple dimensions.

Thus, on the one hand, Sartre declares his unconditional allegiance to Marxism, but to a Marxism rather restricted in content, while, on the other hand, he reintroduces the event, the individual, the autonomy of sociopolitical groups and the irreducibility of the productions of the mind into history. It is true that, according to him, he is merely going back to the original Marxist text. Marxists may be incapable of reading it, but obviously that is their fault, not the fault of Marx. During the Stalinist period particularly, he says, Marxists went in for a sort of voluntarist idealism. Instead of slowly deciphering the complex reality of human history, they proceeded in an arbitrary manner, mechanically applying their interpretative grid without even bothering to acquaint themselves with the facts. They remained ignorant of the multifarious mediations between the production process and actual experience. Marxism is the unsurpassable philosophy of our time but it has become totally sterile in the twentieth century.

The problem is, then, to resuscitate and renew Marxism. Sartre hopes to achieve this not through an original interpretation of the age we live in but through providing Marx's Marxism with a philosophical foundation in existentialism rather than in materialism, or at least in a materialism compatible with existentialism.

Sartre's ambition, as he himself defines it, is to reintroduce man into Marxist knowledge: "He [Sartre] does not, like Kierkegaard reacting against Hegel, contrast the irrational peculiarity of the individual with universal knowledge. But he seeks to reintroduce the unsurpassable peculiarity of human existence into knowledge itself and into the universality of concepts." This statement throws light on the philosophical aim of the author of *L'Etre et le néant,* since events prompted him to move from ontology to *ontic,* from man "as a useless passion" to historical man in search of himself and of truth.

Sartre's attitude toward Marxism involves four kinds of judgment.

1. As far as materialistic metaphysics or objective dialectics

are concerned, he is explicit, categorical, and negative. However strong his desire to cooperate with the Stalinists may have been, he has never made any concessions at the expense of the principles of his own philosophy.

2. As regards Marx's economico-historical sociology, Sartre usually takes the view that it consists of established or self-evident truths. He writes, for instance: "None of these remarks relating to form can, of course, claim to add anything at all to the self-evident truth of the synthetic reconstruction achieved by Marx in *Das Kapital;* they are not even intended to be a marginal commentary on that reconstruction which, precisely because of its self-evident truth, does not admit of any commentary."[5]

This pronouncement, which is hard on the innumerable writers of commentaries, illustrates Sartre's facile acceptance of all those aspects of Marxist thought in which he is not particularly interested, but which were the essential things for Marx himself—for instance, the synthetic reconstruction of capitalism.

3. As regards political action, if it is agreed to apply the term Marxist to the militant members of Communist parties, Sartre has never been a Marxist, although he has been a para-Marxist since 1945. Apart from the short-lived experiment some fifteen years ago of the *Rassemblement démocratique révolutionnaire,* he has been, typically, a fellow traveler. He has never, to the slightest degree, sacrificed his freedom of thought, but he has adopted partisan attitudes which have seemed all the more exasperating through his maintaining that they were not partisan. He has, on occasions, criticized Soviet Russia—for instance, at the time of the Hungarian Revolution—but he has consciously and deliberately applied two different yardsticks. The significance of torture or concentration camps has varied according to the nature of the regime or the party in power. For his own sake, one would have liked the philosopher of freedom to denounce the personality cult before Chairman Khrushchev did so. In spite of his nonconformism, Sartre has not altogether avoided left-wing conformism.

4. This brings us to the final and most interesting aspect of

[5] *Ibid.,* p. 276.

the problem. *La Critique de la raison dialectique* remains within the concepts of historical materialism and the class struggle. The publication of a further volume has already been announced. The aim of the first one is to renew Marxism by reintroducing existence into it, and taking the individual consciousness as the starting point. Sartrian criticism is intended to stand in the same relationship to Marxism as Kantian criticism (according to what we were taught at school) stood in relationship to Newtonian physics. Sartre is endeavoring to demonstrate the possibility of a *single* history which will be the progressive working out of the truth.

In *Critique,* Sartre tends to use the concept of praxis to describe individual action, and he even devotes a few pages to discussing the relationship between the living organism and its setting through the mediation of need. We should not be misled by this change of vocabulary; there is no decisive difference between what he now calls the individual praxis or constituent dialectic and the Being-for-oneself in *L'Etre et le néant.* The individual praxis, like consciousness, is a pro-ject (a throwing forward), at once a retention of the past and a self-translucid transcending of it in the direction of the future, a total apprehension both of the situation and the aim. History would be perfectly dialectical, that is perfectly comprehensible, if it were the history of a single man. It remains intelligible because it is made up of human actions, each of which is comprehensible as an individual praxis or translucid act of consciousness.

The Sartrian dialectic does not begin from the dialogue, that is, from the encounter of the I and the Thou. It is the encounter with the Other which creates a threat to the liberty of each individual. This is not to say that the Other treats me spontaneously as the object of his action and thereby submits me to his will. But since consciousness as praxis is an operative consciousness, the relationship of the individual man with nature and other men through the mediation of fashioned matter (the tool), the risk of alienation is inherent in the relationships between individuals. To be authentically human, these relationships must be founded on reciprocity or equality (both terms

occur in the book). A philosophy which denies the existence
of such a thing as human nature must find some substitute
criterion by which to determine what is to be judged as in-
human. This criterion is reciprocity: The praxis of one person,
in its practical structure and for the accomplishment of its
project, recognizes the praxis of the Other, i.e., in the last resort, it considers the duality of activities as a non-essential characteristic and the unity of the *praxeis* (plural) as such as an
essential characteristic.[6]

In the actual history of mankind, this reciprocity is hardly
ever to be found because of the phenomenon of *scarcity*. What
animal species could be more dangerous for man than an intelligent, skillful species which sets out to deprive me of my means
of livelihood? This animal species is none other than mankind
itself, at once the victim and prisoner of scarcity, which makes
every individual his neighbor's enemy. Thus it is that scarcity,
on which the classical economists founded their theories, brings
us back to Hobbes's vision of mankind: *homo homini lupus.*

History is not governed by necessity. It has its origin and its
intelligible foundation in a contingent fact, coexistent with the
life of our species on this planet: the lack of resources in relation to the number of mouths to be fed. This lack condemns
all societies to eliminate certain of their actual or possible members either after birth or before. An obscure awareness of it is
interiorized in the human consciousness and creates the climate
of scarcity which is, at the same time, the climate of violence in
which all human history takes place.

This first phase of Sartre's critical process is obviously foreign
to the thought not only of Marxists, but also of Engels or
Marx. Neither of them goes back beyond the ancient societies,
i.e., socialized man. The division of labor or violence (prefer-
ably the former) seemed to them to be the source of the class
struggle, which they did not attribute explicitly either to human nature or to a Hegelian dialectical relationship between
master and slave. They were more interested in the historical
mechanism than in the "transcendental deduction" of the class
struggle. However, it does not necessarily follow that the Sar-

6 *Ibid.,* p. 207.

trian conception, on the transcendental level on which it is expressed, is incompatible with Marx's inspiration. At any rate, it allows Sartre to open up an avenue of escape from the hopeless world of *L'Etre et le néant* and *Huis Clos*. Man's inhumanity to man has an ontologically accidental cause. Volume II of *Critique* will presumably take us beyond scarcity and show us the dawn of the age of plenty and of reciprocal consciousness.

Scarcity, which sets the dialectic of history in motion, would not produce such consequences if the freedom of the individual praxis were not immediately threatened by the praxeis of others. Or again, to use a different form of language, each of us is a pro-ject, a total apprehension of our environment in terms of the perceived situation and the end in view. How can innumerable liberties coexist without reciprocal subjugation? The answer is that, as a matter of fact, they cannot, at least not in a world of scarcity: consciousnesses are objectified in their works and this objectification turns into alienation because the opposing consciousnesses deprive it of significance, or distort its significance. All individual freedoms are finally bogged down in what Sartre calls the "practico-inert," the thing-iness of the social organization, to which everyone is subject as if it were a form of physical necessity; it is a necessity which remains intelligible because it derives from the free praxeis of individuals, but it is, in a way, a negation of that liberty.

Jean-Jacques Rousseau wrote: "Man was born free and he is everywhere in chains." According to Sartre, man is free by his very nature, or rather he has no nature because, being free, he decides for himself, but everywhere man is the instrument of man and can nowhere exercise his liberty without violating that of others.

The concept of the *series*, illustrated by the well-known example of the queue of people waiting for the bus at Saint-Germain-des-Prés, characterizes relationships between individuals in their submission to the practico-inert. The members of the queue are together but they do not see each other. They are standing in line, and only the accidental order of their arrival, not the urgency of their journey, will determine the order of their getting into the bus. Each of them is going about his own business and knows nothing of the concerns of the others. They have nothing in common except their need of a means of transport, and the phenomenon of scarcity (there will not be room for all of them) turns them into potential enemies.

It goes without saying that the various collectives that Sartre analyzes in turn are not all as simple as this. Still, even a class is fundamentally only a collective of the serial type. The proletariat, in a state of repose and as an objective entity, is no more than a scattered plurality, subject to internal conflicts and characterized by the enslavement of the free praxeis of individuals not only to the employers or the organization of labor but also to the general context of the practico-inert, of which its innumerable members inevitably form part. How could things be otherwise? Each member of the proletariat is born into a social situation which is not of his own choosing; he interiorizes that objective situation, not because he has lost his freedom but because he has no other way of exercising it. Within the existing framework, the members of the proletariat have, up to a point, a common being, but they are divided precisely by the divisions of society.

Only within a common undertaking do the individual praxeis succeed in overcoming their isolation, their rivalries, and their enslavement one to another and to the general context of the practico-inert. The common undertaking is the collective project, the single goal toward which all the consciousnesses, fused into one and the same action, are striving. A queue at a bus stop symbolizes *serial collectives;* the crowd which stormed the Bastille symbolizes *the group.* At once, there is a reversal of meanings: number, which in the collectives was a source of dispersal, solitude and enslavement, becomes a factor of confidence and dynamic action. The crowd storming the Bastille has only one soul and, as it were, only one consciousness. The proletariat is a form of being, an *exis,* in which the individual consciousnesses participate but within which they are alienated; the active group, the crowd storming the Bastille, restores their lost liberty to the individual praxeis.

Thus the fusion of individuals within a revolutionary crowd becomes a symbol of collective liberation.

We cannot storm a new Bastille every day. Although I am fighting side by side with my fellow campaigners today, I have not renounced my freedom. Tomorrow I may betray them, or at least I cannot be sure that I shall not be involved in a betrayal: my own freedom does not allow me to dispose of my future. I cannot but mistrust myself, and that is why the group can only be formed by each member pledging himself to grant the others the right to punish him if he breaks his word. The group demands a pledge and calls for the exercise of terror. Threatened by external enemies and still more so by internal decomposition, it survives as an expression of will power and as an active agent, thanks to the freely granted submission of all its members to the requirements of the common undertaking.

The proletariat as a group emerges from the class as a collective by, and in, action. But the group, once it has come into being, is subject in its turn to the obligations of social existence. It, too, must share out tasks, differentiate between functions, assign each individual to his appropriate place and exact obedience. It, too, is in danger of degenerating into that inertia against which it revolted. It, too, must evolve its institutions and became a quasi organism, i.e., lose the translucidity of the two fully comprehensible praxeis, that of the single individual and that of the fused group (the crowd storming the Bastille).

This being so, in what way is the institutionalized group to be distinguished from the collectives which went to make up the practico-inert? It remains different from them insofar as it retains something of the single manifestation of will power which gave rise to the undertaking, and insofar as the members of the group do not forget the vow of fidelity by which they are bound.

The dialectic of the series and the group, of the practico-inert and revolutionary praxis, is obviously Sartrian, not Marxist. It supposes that individual action is the only dialectical and practical reality, the motive force behind everything, and that the act of revolt is, as it were, "the beginning of humanity."

But although it claims not to be in conflict with the Marxist vision of historical becoming, such a dialectic suggests instead an endless alternation of alienation and revolution. Individuals allow themselves to be gradually caught within a social order more and more comparable to physical necessity, then reassert their human dignity through revolt and organize a revolution which, in its turn, once it has been institutionalized, will fall back into inertia and lose that single force of will power which alone differentiated it from the practico-inert.

The theory of the group, and the contrast between the working class as a collective entity and the revolutionary group as praxis, might be considered as a philosophical justification of Bolshevik practice and of the substitution of the party for the class as the subject of history. But I do not think that this kind of justification would reassure ideologists in Moscow or Peking.

Admittedly, Sartre explains that the Stalinist phase was inevitable.

Historical experience has undoubtedly shown that the initial phase of socialist society in course of construction, considered on the still abstract level of power, could only be an indissoluble aggregation of bureaucracy, terror, and the personality cult.[7]

This sentence will arouse the indignation of some readers, because it puts the stamp of historical necessity on a historical phenomenon which is still dripping with fresh blood. However, it strikes me as being mainly naïve. I am not much impressed by retrospective demonstrations tending to prove that what has happened could not have turned out otherwise. Any philosopher of talent can successfully undertake such demonstrations, provided, of course, he is not called upon to apply the method to the future. As for the orthodox thinkers in Moscow and Peking, they cannot welcome the heretical idea which introduces the demonstration just summarized:

[7] *Ibid.*, p. 630.

The reason why the dictatorship of the proletariat has never, at any moment, occurred—as the actual exercising of power through the totalization of the working class—is that the very notion is absurd, since it is a bastard compromise between the active and sovereign group and passive seriality.

What hope of renewal does the *Critique* hold out for Marxism? To establish a radical distinction, as Sartre does, between analytical and dialectical reason, between the natural sciences and the study of man, between the unintelligibility of natural phenomena and the intrinsic intelligibility of history is to break not only with the Marxism of Lenin and Engels but also with that of Marx himself. The repeated statement that the individual praxis is the final condition of intelligibility, the only practical and dialectical reality, imposes on a philosophy which aims at a total interpretation of history a task that Sartre himself, in spite of his efforts, cannot bring to completion.

How can all the varieties of lived experience be fitted into Marxist knowledge without it being disrupted or the experiences themselves being blurred? If authentic reality is made up only of men, their actions, their sufferings or their dreams, how can their individual existences, each of which is unique and irreplaceable, be totalized? How can one pass from these multifarious points of view—since each individual sees history from his particular angle—to a single truth, which would constitute a system of knowledge and would not eliminate individuals from the realm of thought as pitilessly as wars and revolutions eliminate them from the world of fact? Why should the formal and static dialectics of the practico-inert and of action, of the series and the group, come to an end before the end of scarcity? As a matter of fact, Sartre himself seems to doubt whether his dialectic can come to an end, and (in the conclusion to a note on p. 349) he asks the question: "Will the disappearance of capitalist forms of alienation be synonymous with the abolition of all forms of alienation?" He may well ask; the answer is not necessarily in the affirmative.

It is pointless to inquire whether or not the thought of one philosopher is in agreement with that of another. It has obviously not been my intention to grant, or refuse, Sartre the right to call himself a Marxist; in any case, my authorization would be neither here nor there. I wanted to point out to what an extent he has remained unchanged. This is not to say that *L'Etre et le néant* foreshadows *La Critique de la raison dialectique*. On the contrary, the latter marks a distinct development in relation to the former, and each reader must decide for himself whether it is to be considered as progress or decline.

In one place only does Sartre explicitly reject a point of view put forward in *L'Etre et le néant:* "Fundamental alienation is not, as *L'Etre et le néant* might wrongly lead the reader to suppose, an effect of prenatal choice: it is an effect of the univocal relationship of interiority uniting man, as a practical organism, to his environment."[8] Alienation, like the conflict of consciousnesses, must have its origin in society; otherwise we find ourselves going back to Hobbes, not to Marx. But since Sartre accepts Marx's concrete interpretations of actual history wholeheartedly and uncritically, he concentrates all his energies on a phenomenologico-existential analysis, which is concerned only with the Hegelian elements in Marxist thought and is, above all, typically Sartrian. It is a subtle and bitter analysis, charged with resentment and abstract generosity, distinguished by a sometimes admirable, sometimes exasperating, verbal virtuosity, and occasionally too simple in the opposites it postulates: in fact the life of men in society oscillates inevitably between the series and the group, between alienation and freedom; according to circumstances, the humanization of the relationships between individuals—the impulse toward reciprocity between the praxeis—calls for violence or can be reconciled with reformism.

I do not think that Sartre has achieved his aim of renewing Marxism which, in the hands of the Stalinists, congealed into a sterile dogmatism. Marx's inspiration and method are today an integral part of the collective consciousness and continue to bear fruit. In Moscow and in the so-called People's Democracies, a body of doctrine, an ideological catechism, has been raised to the level of a state truth. The Marxist-Leninists who,

8 *L'Etre et le néant*, p. 288.

willingly or unwillingly, subscribe to this state truth, are quite consistent in rejecting the *Critique,* because it expresses a slightly Marxianized Sartrism or—if a different formulation is preferred—a Marxism that has been recast in the Sartrian mode.

The critical process carried out in these 755 pages may interest philosophers, but it is not very helpful to sociologists, economists, and historians, who find in it either well-known ideas translated into a difficult vocabulary or categorical assertions relating to some mysterious dialectical reason, in the absence of which, says Sartre, "nothing that is said or written about ourselves and our fellow men, either in the East or the West—not a sentence, not a single word—can be anything other than grossly mistaken."

It goes without saying that I myself must be involved in this wholesale condemnation, but since I have to conclude, I shall do so in the manner which, according to Simone de Beauvoir in *The Prime of Life,* was characteristic of me during our interminable discussions when we were young. Sartre cannot have it both ways. If he is trying to renew the Marxism-Leninism of Moscow and Peking, he is wasting his time, because state truths or official ideologies obey their own laws, which are not those of the free inquiry practiced by Sartre himself. If he wants to renew Marxist thought in the West, he should model himself on Marx, that is, analyze the capitalist *and* socialist societies of the twentieth century, as Marx analyzed the capitalist societies of the nineteenth century. Marxism cannot be renewed by going back from *Das Kapital* to the *Economic and Philosophic Manuscripts,* or by trying to achieve some impossible reconciliation between Kierkegaard and Marx.

In short, it would be better to write the *Das Kapital* of the twentieth century, instead of proclaiming allegiance to the *Das Kapital* of the nineteenth.

Epilogue[*]

IT IS the thesis of *World Perspectives* that man is in the process of developing a new consciousness which, in spite of his apparent spiritual and moral captivity, can eventually lift the human race above and beyond the fear, ignorance, and isolation which beset it today. It is to this nascent consciousness, to this concept of man born out of a universe perceived through a fresh vision of reality, that *World Perspectives* is dedicated.

Only those spiritual and intellectual leaders of our epoch who have a paternity in this extension of man's horizons are invited to participate in this Series: those who are aware of the truth that beyond the divisiveness among men there exists a primordial unitive power since we are all bound together by a common humanity more fundamental than any unity of dogma; those who recognize that the centrifugal force which has scattered and atomized mankind must be replaced by an integrating structure and process capable of bestowing meaning and purpose on existence; those who realize that science itself, when not inhibited by the limitations of its own methodology, when chastened and humbled, commits man to an indeterminate range of yet undreamed consequences that may flow from it.

This Series endeavors to point to a reality of which scientific theory has revealed only one aspect. It is the commitment to this reality that lends universal intent to a scientist's most original and solitary thought. By acknowledging this frankly we shall restore science to the great family of human aspirations by which men hope to fulfill themselves in the world community as thinking and sentient beings. For our problem is to discover a principle of differentiation and yet relationship

[*] Published in its original hardcover edition by Harper & Row as Volume Forty of the *World Perspectives* Series, planned and edited by Ruth Nanda Anshen.

lucid enough to justify and to purify scientific, philosophic and all other knowledge, both discursive and intuitive, by accepting their interdependence. This is the crisis in consciousness made articulate through the crisis in science. This is the new awakening.

Each volume presents the thought and belief of its author and points to the way in which religion, philosophy, art, science, economics, politics and history may constitute that form of human activity which takes the fullest and most precise account of variousness, possibility, complexity and difficulty. Thus *World Perspectives* endeavors to define that ecumenical power of the mind and heart which enables man through his mysterious greatness to re-create his life.

This series is committed to a re-examination of all those sides of human endeavor which the specialist was taught to believe he could safely leave aside. It interprets present and past events impinging on human life in our growing World Age and envisages what man may yet attain when summoned by an unbending inner necessity to the quest of what is most exalted in him. Its purpose is to offer new vistas in terms of world and human development while refusing to betray the intimate correlation between universality and individuality, dynamics and form, freedom and destiny. Each author deals with the increasing realization that spirit and nature are not separate and apart; that intuition and reason must regain their importance as the means of perceiving and fusing inner being with outer reality.

World Perspectives endeavors to show that the conception of wholeness, unity, organism is a higher and more concrete conception than that of matter and energy. Thus an enlarged meaning of life, of biology, not as it is revealed in the test tube of the laboratory but as it is experienced within the organism of life itself, is attempted in this Series. For the principle of life consists in the tension which connects spirit with the realm of matter, symbiotically joined. The element of life is dominant in the very texture of nature, thus rendering life, biology, a transempirical science. The laws of life have their origin beyond their mere physical manifestations and compel us to consider their spiritual source. In fact, the widening of the conceptual framework has not only served to restore order within the respective branches of knowledge, but has also disclosed analogies in man's position regarding the analysis and synthesis of experience in apparently separated domains of knowledge suggesting the possibility of an ever more embracing objective description of the meaning of life.

Knowledge, it is shown in these books, no longer consists in a manipulation of man and nature as opposite forces, nor in the reduction of data to mere statistical order, but is a means of liberating mankind from the destructive power of fear, pointing the way toward the goal of the rehabilitation of the human will and the rebirth of faith and confidence in the human person. The works published also endeavor to reveal that the cry for patterns, systems and authorities is growing less insistent as the desire grows stronger in both East and West for the recovery of a dignity, integrity and self-realization which are the inalienable rights of man who may now guide change by means of conscious purpose in the light of rational experience.

Other vital questions explored relate to problems of international understanding as well as to problems dealing with prejudice and the resultant tensions and antagonisms. The growing perception and responsibility of our World Age point to the new reality that the individual person and the collective person supplement and integrate each other; that the thrall of totalitarianism of both left and right has been shaken in the universal desire to recapture the authority of truth and human totality. Mankind can finally place its trust not in a proletarian authoritarianism, not in a secularized humanism, both of which have betrayed the spiritual property right of history, but in a sacramental brotherhood and in the unity of knowledge. This new consciousness has created a widening of human horizons beyond every parochialism, and a revolution in human thought comparable to the basic assumption, among the ancient Greeks, of the sovereignty of reason; corresponding to the great effulgence of the moral conscience articulated by the Hebrew prophets; analogous to the fundamental assertions of Christianity; or to the beginning of a new scientific era, the era of the science of dynamics, the experimental foundations of which were laid by Galileo in the Renaissance.

An important effort of this Series is to re-examine the contradictory meanings and applications which are given today to such terms as democracy, freedom, justice, love, peace, brotherhood and God. The purpose of such inquiries is to clear the way for the foundation of a genuine *world* history not in terms of nation or race or culture but in terms of man in relation to God, to himself, his fellow man and the universe, that reach beyond immediate self-interest. For the meaning of the World Age consists in respecting man's hopes and dreams which lead to a deeper understanding of the basic values of all peoples.

World Perspectives is planned to gain insight into the meaning of man, who not only is determined by history but who also determines history. History is to be understood as concerned not only with the life of man on this planet but as including also such cosmic influences as interpenetrate our human world. This generation is discovering that history does not conform to the social optimism of modern civilization and that the organization of human communities and the establishment of freedom and peace are not only intellectual achievements but spiritual and moral achievements as well, demanding a cherishing of the wholeness of human personality, the "unmediated wholeness of feeling and thought," and constituting a never-ending challenge to man, emerging from the abyss of meaninglessness and suffering, to be renewed and replenished in the totality of his life.

Justice itself, which has been "in a state of pilgrimage and crucifixion" and now is being slowly liberated from the grip of social and political demonologies in the East as well as in the West, begins to question its own premises. The modern revolutionary movements which have challenged the sacred institutions of society by protecting social injustice in the name of social justice are here examined and re-evaluated.

In the light of this, we have no choice but to admit that the *un*freedom against which freedom is measured must be retained with it, namely, that the aspect of truth out of which the night view appears to emerge, the darkness of our time, is as little abandonable as is man's subjective advance. Thus the two sources of man's consciousness are inseparable, not as dead but as living and complementary, an aspect of that "principle of complementarity" through which Niels Bohr has sought to unite the quantum and the wave, both of which constitute the very fabric of life's radiant energy.

There is in mankind today a counterforce to the sterility and danger of a quantitative, anonymous mass culture; a new, if sometimes imperceptible, spiritual sense of convergence toward world unity on the basis of the sacredness of each human person and respect for the plurality of cultures. There is a growing awareness that equality may not be evaluated in mere numerical terms but is proportionate and analogical in its reality. For when equality is equated with interchangeability, individuality is negated and the human person extinguished.

We stand at the brink of an age of a world in which human life presses forward to actualize new forms. The false separation of man and nature, of time and space, of freedom and security, is acknowledged, and we are faced with a new vision of man in his organic unity and of history offering a richness and diversity of quality and majesty of scope hitherto unprecedented. In relating the accumulated wisdom of man's spirit to the new reality of the World Age, in articulating its thought and belief, *World Perspectives* seeks to encourage a renaissance of hope in society and of pride in man's decision as to what his destiny will be.

World Perspectives is committed to the recognition that all great changes are preceded by a vigorous intellectual re-evaluation and reorganization. Our authors are aware that the sin of *hubris* may be avoided by showing that the creative process itself is not a free activity if by free we mean arbitrary, or unrelated to cosmic law. For the creative process in the human mind, the developmental process in organic nature and the basic laws of the inorganic realm may be but varied expressions of a universal formative process. Thus *World Perspectives* hopes to show that although the present apocalyptic period is one of exceptional tensions, there is also at work an exceptional movement toward a compensating unity which refuses to violate the ultimate moral power at work in the universe, that very power upon which all human effort must at last depend. In this way we may come to understand that there exists an inherent independence of spiritual and mental growth which, though conditioned by circumstances, is never determined by circumstances. In this way the great plethora of human knowledge may be correlated with an insight into the nature of human nature by being attuned to the wide and deep range of human thought and human experience.

In spite of the infinite obligation of men and in spite of their finite power, in spite of the intransigence of nationalisms, and in spite of the homelessness of moral passions rendered ineffectual by the scientific outlook, beneath the apparent turmoil and upheaval of the present, and out of the transformations of this dynamic period with the unfolding of a world consciousness, the purpose of *World Perspectives* is to help quicken the "unshaken heart of well-rounded truth" and interpret the significant elements of the World Age now taking shape out of the core of that undimmed continuity of the creative process which restores man to mankind while deepening and enhancing his communion with the universe.

RUTH NANDA ANSHEN

ABOUT THE AUTHOR

Raymond Aron was born in Paris in 1905. From 1955 to 1968 he was Professor of Sociology at the Faculté des Lettres et des Sciences Humaines of the University of Paris. In 1960 he became Director of the École Pratique des Hautes Études. He has been a visiting professor at Cornell University and Harvard University and is an honorary member of the American Academy of Arts and Sciences.

During World War II, Professor Aron was Editor-in-Chief of *La France Libre,* published in London, and since 1947 has been a columnist for *Le Figaro.* He is the author of *The Great Debate, The Dawn of Universal History, France: the New Republic, German Sociology, Introduction to the Philosophy of History, The Opium of the Intellectuals, Peace and War: A Theory of International Relations,* and *The Industrial Society.*